# What Others Say About This Book

*Getting Beyond Tragedy* is a straightforward, transparent story of how one family experienced, endured and continues moving beyond a tragedy. In this case the tragedy was the death of the youngest of three children.

The father, a minister of the Presbyterian Church (USA), reveals his struggle honestly and vulnerably through his poetry. Expressions of powerful, gut-wrenching feelings call forth empathetic responses, and the reader identifies with the suffering anguish and the abiding trust, with the foreboding desperation and the eternal hope, and with the prevailing sadness and the abiding love enfleshed in this parent/pastor.

The mother, an older sister, and a brother reflect on how this family tragedy has formed their characters, reformed their faith, and forged their vocational choices. Getting beyond this tragedy required suffering with hope in God for each member of this family. In their respective ways they learned experientially that suffering without hope produces resentment and despair. But hope without suffering creates illusions and naivete. With courage and perseverance they grieved their loss and trusted both Scott and themselves to the God of hope.

Those espousing the faith of the Judeo-Christian community will be informed, and perhaps reformed, by the chapter entitled "Tragedy and the Will of God." Succinctly stated, Reverend Noble concludes: "(Is) tragedy good? No. But with God working with us in tragedy, at least some good can come from it. That may be tragedy's only redeeming feature."

Persons enduring a tragedy will be encouraged to move beyond their present struggle. Those who are getting beyond their tragedy will experience communion with this family. Ministers and other helping professionals will discover an enabling resource for their lending library. Anyone grieving losses can identify with the inescapable process described by the Noble family in *Getting Beyond Tragedy*.

—THE REV. JASPER N. KEITH, JR., TH.D.
Pastor, Decatur Presbyterian Church
Professor Emeritus, Columbia Theological Seminary


N o parent ever expects to be forced to witness the profound suffering of his own child at the hands of a deadly disease like cancer. Certainly, nothing can prepare one for such an experience. Cancer happens to other people. It happens to adults, not children. Doesn't it?

Dr. Noble, through his powerful work, tells us that cancer can and does happen to children. And sometimes, the cancer wins and the child dies. How does a parent survive such a loss—the most supreme loss imaginable? How does his faith survive when his greatest love, his innocent child, has been robbed of life on earth by a vicious disease?

As a mother of a child who was diagnosed with cancer at only five weeks old, I read *Getting Beyond Tragedy* with intense interest. I hoped to find in these pages the answers to the questions that have haunted me into the late hours of the night. Why do children get cancer? Why must they suffer? Through my own journey with childhood cancer, I had come to accept that only God knows the answers to these questions, and the choice I affirmatively made was to believe in the face of these difficult questions. But my acceptance of God as our loving Father never erased the lingering questions: Why does our God allow tragedy? Why must it touch our children?

Dr. Noble bravely and generously allows us into the immense tragedy of all who knew and loved his precious son, Scott. Although we long to comfort Dr. Noble as a grieving, loving father, he comforts us, instead, through his thoughtful, honest words. He does not try to answer our questions with glib, trite answers. Instead, he admits what we cannot know but brings comfort and peace to our hearts by bringing forward Proverbs 3:5-6: We must trust in the Lord with all our hearts and not lean on our own understanding.

While *Getting Beyond Tragedy* does not answer *the* question of *why*, because it cannot, it reminds us that in the depths of our anguish, we cannot rely on our own understanding, but we must trust in the Lord with all our hearts. If we do, and as God works through us, our tragedy will not be in vain—some good will come from it. As a mother of a child with cancer, this is a message with deep value to be remembered time and time again as the tragic circumstance of childhood cancer repeats itself. I am grateful to Dr. Noble for providing me, through his work, comfort I need.

—Kristin Connor
Attorney-at-law and Senior VP, CureSearch National Childhood Cancer Foundation

*Also by James Phillips Noble*

BEYOND THE BURNING BUS:
THE CIVIL RIGHTS REVOLUTION IN A SOUTHERN TOWN

FIFTEEN POEMS FOR THOSE ATTAINING
THREE SCORE AND TEN YEARS

# GETTING BEYOND TRAGEDY

*A Minister's Search for Answers*
*to the 'Why, God?' Question*
*Which Torments Grieving Families*

JAMES PHILLIPS NOBLE

MBF PRESS
Montgomery

Designed for the Noble family by Randall Williams

Trade paper ISBN-13: 978-0-9785311-0-2
Trade paper ISBN-10: 0-9785311-0-8
Limited trade cloth printing

Printed in the United States of America

THE REVEREND J. PHILLIPS NOBLE grew up in
Learned, Mississippi. After graduating from King
College in Bristol, Tennessee, and Columbia
Theological Seminary in Decatur, Georgia, he was
ordained a Presbyterian minister. Graduate work
was done in Edinburgh, Scotland, and Cambridge
University in England. Over his career, he served
pastorates in Alabama, Georgia, and South Carolina. Noble was also Co-President of the Board of
Pensions of the Presbyterian Church, USA. He
has traveled extensively on six continents. Noble
is married to Betty Pope Scott. They have three
children and two grandchildren. He is retired and
living in Decatur, Georgia.

TO THE MEMORY OF

MILTON SCOTT NOBLE

1954–1968

# CONTENTS

# PREFACE

Tragedy. It is no respecter of persons. There are millions of people all over the world into whose lives tragedy has come. When the poet Longfellow wrote, "Into each life some rain must fall / Some days must be dark and dreary," it is a statement far too mild for tragedy. Tragedy is the striking of lightning, the roar of a tornado, the ripping off of the roof, the shattering of walls and the shaking of the foundations. When tragedy comes everything changes. Nothing remains the same.

It often comes without warning. It just suddenly dumps its load on unsuspecting persons. When driving through the mountains there are two signs often seen along the highway. One reads, "Beware of Fallen Rocks" and the other reads, "Beware of Falling Rocks."

One can watch out for rocks that have fallen on to the highway and usually avoid them. But "falling rocks" is different. How does one look out for "falling rocks"? They just come crashing down without warning. That is the way it is with much tragedy. We do not cause it. We do not know that it is coming or when it is coming. All at once we are struck by tragedy.

We are numb. The impact of it is so strong. How will we survive? What will we do? Then when we get over the first shock of it, the one word question explodes in our minds: WHY? If we believe in God at all, it immediately becomes a God question. Why did God let it happen? If God is a God of love, why did God let it happen? If God is all powerful AND God of love, then really why? The tsunami tragedy at the end of 2004 surfaced this question in all religions—it is clearly a universal question. It is probably as deep into theology as one will ever get.

Tragedy wears many faces and comes in many forms. It may creep in on quiet feet as well as burst in suddenly. It has been quietly developing, but then the doctor says, "Cancer," and we are suddenly face to face with a beast. A telephone may ring and a voice say, "there has been a wreck." There is a telegram that says, "Your son in the service . . ." One night your mate of ten years says, "I want a divorce." From the delivery room, the doctor says, "You have a son or a daughter, but . . ."

The world is filled with people who are no stranger to tragedy. Some people get beyond it very well. Some have great difficulty in recovering; some never do. Tragedy nearly always leaves its mark, but sometimes it leaves one crippled in various ways.

When tragedy strikes it ultimately becomes a question of how we get beyond tragedy. There is no simple and easy answer. I am always skeptical about the academic and theological answers of someone who has never experienced tragedy. One does not know until one has been there. Having been there does not mean that one has simple and easy answers, or answers at all, but at least there is a note of reality in their thinking and feeling.

THERE ARE THREE PARTS to this book, which are presented here out of the order in which they were written. Our thirteen-year-old son had leukemia in 1967 and died from it a year and a half later.

Part of my therapy was the writing of a poetic expression of my feelings, thoughts, and experiences as I faced the reality of the tragedy of Scott's sufferings and death. My family and I struggled to find a way through it and a lot (not all) of the struggle is revealed in the poetry.

This becomes the middle part of the book. It is hoped there will be some insights there that will be helpful to others who experience a tragedy like this, or another kind of tragedy. To emerge in the sunlight on the other side of tragedy is an aim and goal worth striving for. It is not easy, but it is possible.

The first and third parts of the book were written almost forty years after Scott's death. The part which comes first in the order of the book is a brief theological reflection, "Tragedy and the Will of God."

It was written after almost fifty years of my pastoral work of being with people who have experienced many forms of tragedy. It emerges from a life-long study of the Bible and reflections on the meaning of the Christian faith. It rejects the glib and easy assignment of the will of God to tragedies that occur.

There are people who, observing tragedy in other peoples' lives, attempt to give comfort to those experiencing tragedy, by saying, "It is the will of God." As well-meaning as such people are, often such a statement increases the already heavy load one is bearing if they are told that the God of love whom they worship wanted or willed this tragedy to happen. The reflection on "Tragedy and the Will of God" gives what may be a fresh and new expression of a better way to experience faith in God in the midst of tragedy. Hopefully it will help many who experience tragedy to find their way into the sunlight of God's love and care and to a fulfilling life after tragedy, even if the mark of the tragedy remains.

The final part of the book consists of reflections on Scott's life by his mother, brother, and sister. These are obviously deeply personal and are part of the memorial to Scott's memory which we all wanted this book to be.

Betty and Phil were teenagers at the time of Scott's death, and here they have shared their personal experiences as they witnessed the suffering of their brother, and tell how their lives were and still are impacted by those exeriences.

Betty, now a school and counseling psychologist, gives her life in working with people, especially children. She specializes in working with children of divorce, as well as children with school problems, such as learning disabilities and attention problems. Many of the children and adult clients she sees often are dealing with tragedies of some sort.

As she indicates, the experience with Scott has greatly affected her life and was responsible to a great extent in leading her to dedicate her life to helping children and others facing problems. In her office she has the following poem, which says a lot about her commitment and motivation:

> A hundred years from now
> it will not matter what my bank account was,
> the sort of house I lived in,
> or the kind of car I drove—
> but, the world may be different
> because I was important
> in the life of a child.
>                         —FOREST WITCRAFT

While Betty helps people "one on one," Phil, Jr. has a desire to help people, especially the poor and disadvantaged, through structures and systems of society that affect people in mass. His desire to work through the political process to change or improve these systems to help people who are suffering by discrimination and neglect has been impacted by Scott's suffering and death.

Scott's early death was, and is, a heavy tragedy that makes no sense. As the great Scottish theologian William Barclay said, the most unexplainable tragedy of all is the death of a child. Yet without in any way denying the reality of that tragedy, out of it has come, at least, two lives that have been remarkably influenced by it and their lives set on a course to help others in need.

There are many, many, others whose lives have been influenced by a tragedy in their experience and as a result have lived more useful lives than they would have if they had not experienced tragedy. This is a vivid example of the truth that "in everything [even tragedy] God works for good with those who love him."

Tragedy good? No. But with God working with us in tragedy, at least some good can come from it. That may be tragedy's only redeeming feature.

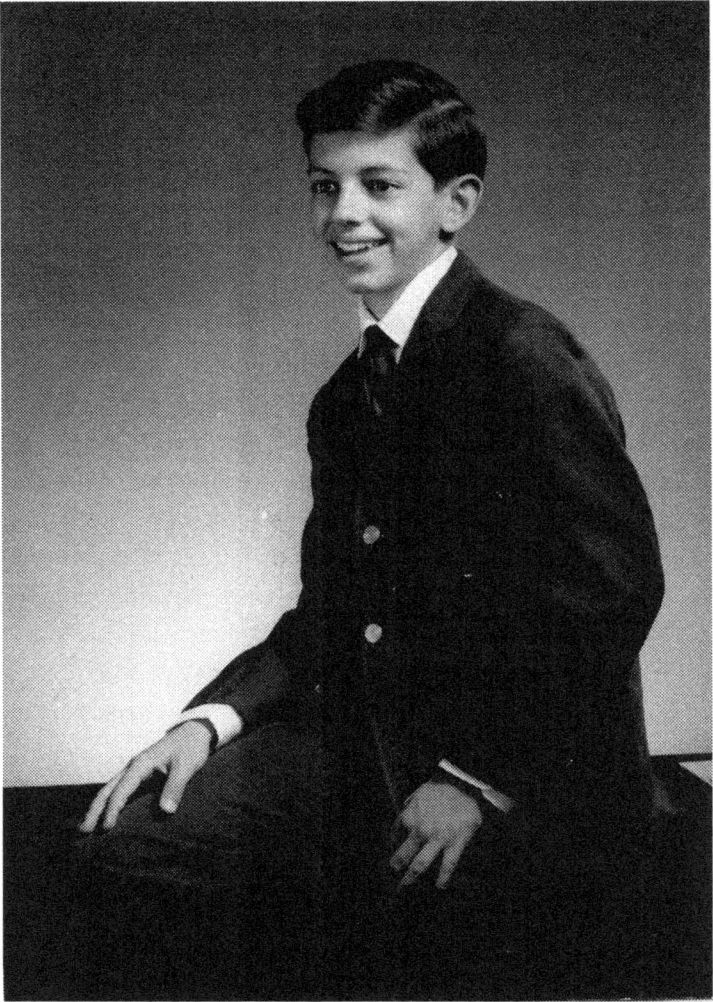

MILTON SCOTT NOBLE
*March 1967, twelve years old*

*Part One*
# ON TRAGEDY

# 1

# TRAGEDY AND THE
# WILL OF GOD

The oldest book in the Bible is the story of a man named Job struggling with a series of tragedies; loss of property, loss of loved ones, loss of health, and agonizingly asking WHY? And WHERE IS GOD? Ancient playwrights wrote Tragedies that were performed in amphitheaters in Athens and Rome, and the same two questions were there. Every newspaper printed this very day in a hundred different languages carries stories of human tragedy and in their wake are the same two agonizing questions: Why? And where is God?

Not all tragedies result in the same kind of "Whys." When a person smokes three packs of cigarettes a day for forty years and then has cancer, there is not a "Why" question. But when someone has observed all the rules of good health all their lives and at age fifty a fatal illness occurs, the "Why" question is a big one. When an immature teenager drinks too much alcohol and then drives a car too fast, and an accident occurs, the "Why" question is not a major one. But when a young father with his wife and two children drives into his driveway and a large tree limb falls on the car killing his wife and two children, the "Why" question as well as the "Where is God" question is huge. In between the tragedies where the thing that caused them is obvious and where there is no apparent reason is a large gray area.

Tragedy is tragedy whenever and however it occurs. Some are more understandable than others. The less understandable they are the more intense are the "Why" and "Where is God" questions. However, the experience of tragedy almost universally brings these two questions. If you have experienced tragedy my guess is that you have been relentlessly pounded by these two questions. The agony relating to the questions usually abates with the passing of time, but seldom goes away entirely. They are well-nigh unanswerable questions. The questions are like this: Where is God in this? Is this what God willed? If God be a God of love, why did God let such a tragedy happen?

If simple and easy answers are given, we can almost be sure they are wrong. But faith does help us as we keep reaching out for elusive answers. The apostle Paul put tragedy and God together in a powerful verse in his letter to the Romans. It does not tie up answers in a neat package, but it may give us a clue and point us in a direction that may ultimately bring us some relief. "We know that in everything [and that includes tragedy] God works for good with those who love God—" (Romans 8:28 Revised Standard Version). They are mere words, but may become dynamic when set in the human experience. I deliberately use the word "may." There are no "cut and dried" assurances.

I fully realize that this does not answer all the "God" questions that come when tragedy strikes. What about the omnipotent God? What about the all-powerful God that can do any and every thing? Why does God not heal or prevent the tragedy? There are many mysteries. But I believe one can live with these unanswerable questions, better than one can live with the concept that suffering and tragedy is what the God of fatherly love wants or wills for his children. Indeed, Jesus said, "It is not the will of my Father who is in heaven that one of these little ones should perish" (Matthew 18:14 Revised Standard Version).

Setting these ideas in the context of actual human stories may be illuminating. I was the young minister of the Second Presbyterian Church in Greenville, South Carolina, in the years following World War II, 1947-1956. One day I made an appointment and went to see an elderly couple who had been attending our Church. They were Episcopalians who had asked me to come visit them. He had graying and thinning hair. Her gray hair was in a knot at the back of her head. They were good, gentle, and humble people. Sitting in their living room, we had a delightful visit about a number of things. I thought they were interested in the Church, possibly considering joining the Second Presbyterian Church.

In the process of the visit they pointed out a picture of their son on the table in the living room. It was a picture of a fine-looking young man. He had been killed a few years earlier in World War II. They talked about it a bit. He was their only son. They were now left in their older years without any children or family, and they really were at a loss to understand it. They did not say all of that at the time; they simply shared the fact that he had been killed in the war.

We talked about some other things, and then came the significant question. They said to me, "Do you believe that everything that happens is for the best?" As I have already said I was a young minister having been ordained to the ministry only four years earlier. I may not have had much judgment or sense in those days, but I had enough to recognize that that question carried a lot of freight! For one thing they were still feeling the agony of the death of their only son in the war. And it was apparent that they were still wondering why, having only one son, it would happen? Now they were left alone, and in their lingering hurt it made no sense to them.

They had been attending the Second Presbyterian Church, and they knew that Presbyterians believe in predestination. They probably had heard people say, "Everything that happens is for the best." Their questioning had to do not only with their experience, but with the viewpoint of the Presbyterian Church, and larger than that, the viewpoint of Christian faith about the interpretation of a tragedy such as they had experienced.

I probably did not do a good job of answering. I sensed the poignant sorrow that was still with them. I was mindful of the King James Version of Romans 8:28, having learned it before seminary days, and having talked about it in seminary classes. That verse reads, "We know that all things work together for good to them that love God." I sensed that I could not easily say to them that everything happens for the best. But that verse was there which seemed to imply that everything did happen for the best, and it troubled me. I did not really know how to deal with it.

It was years later when I discovered a different version of Romans 8:28, the translation that is in the Revised Standard Version. When put side by side the translations sound very similar, yet there is a vast difference in the two. The King James Version reads, "And we know that all things work together for good to them that love God." The Revised Standard Version reads, "We know that in everything God works for good with those who love God."

The King James Version seems to imply that everything that happens is for good and is for the best. It can be taken to mean that no matter how tragic, no matter how bad something is, it is for the best. The Revised Standard Version says, no matter what happens, God can work in it to bring good out of it. There is a vast difference in the two versions. The King James Version implies that whatever happens is good. The Revised Standard Version permits the recognition of the reality, the awful reality, of tragedy and yet suggests that somehow, though unseen now, God being with me in the tragedy may even in time bring good out of it. The tragedy is not recognized as good. It is horrible, but God is with us and some good may come from it.

Put the experience of the elderly couple in that context. They were unable to understand why the only son they had would be taken in war. Rightly, they were reluctant to blame that on God, or to conclude that it was God's will. But they struggled with the meaning of why it happened. If I had known the Revised Standard Version's translation and could have said to them, "God doesn't want suffering and senseless death and God suffers with you in it and he has promised to be with us in tragedy and loss," I think they could have been helped by that truth, and furthermore, I believe it would have been closer to Biblical truth.

When one says that everything works for good, it is very near saying "Everything that happens is the will of God." That has God approving of some of the most horrible deeds of mankind that one can imagine, or the most horrible tragedies that can happen. Nowhere has that been said more clearly than in a short article I discovered some time ago. The language of its unknown author is stronger than I would want to use, but I think in essence it is speaking the Biblical truth:

> Some time ago when a noted medical missionary was killed
> by guerrillas in Africa, his father in the United States told re-
> porters that he was sustained in his sorrow by his belief that his

son's death was "the will of God." The reporters accepted this statement as evidence of a "strong religious faith." One need not doubt that faith to affirm that the death of the missionary doctor was no more the will of God than the vast abomination of Hitler's extermination camps was the will of God.

The conviction that God can, and does, use and overrule for good the most dreadful deeds, does not imply that the deeds themselves are the will of God. Blasphemy—that is to say, profane speaking about God—has almost lost meaning to the modern mind. But, if there be any blasphemy remaining, it must be the accusation that the monstrous iniquities which in our lifetime have deluged the earth with pain and death are the work not of evil men but of a capricious and inscrutable God.

When a little child is run over by a drunken driver, or assaulted by a sexually deranged adult, it is religious hypocrisy for parents to murmur about the submission to the will of God. The believer should meet his sorrow not in numbed resignation that this is what God wanted, but in renewed commitment to the God and Father of Jesus Christ, whose will—as Christ said—is that not one of these little ones should perish.

There is a vast difference in saying that whatever happens is what God wants or is for the best, and in saying *no matter what happens God will be with us* in that experience and may even bring good out of it. This is not an academic exercise, but it touches every one of us at some point in our lives or will touch us when tragedy strikes.

On Christmas day of 1966, the day our twelve-year-old son, Scott, was to make his public profession of faith and unite with the Church with a group of his peers, he fainted and was carried out of the sanctuary in the strong arms of an Elder of the

Church who was also a doctor. It was the first sign of an illness that led to the discovery of a cancerous tumor in his chest which the doctors said was lymphosarcoma.

In January Scott had an operation. The surgeon was not able to remove the lymphosarcoma. There followed several weeks of radiation treatment. At the end of March—March the thirtieth to be exact, his mother's birthday—it was discovered that he had leukemia. From the end of March until the next Easter (1968), we fought the disease with all the treatments available to medical science. He died on Black Saturday of 1968 and was buried on Monday after Easter. During those months, my wife and I and our other two children recognized the deep suffering that Scott went through in all of the experience of that disease.

During that period of time I agonized days and nights about why, but one of the things that bothered me most was that a God whom I called Father and whom I believed loved me as a father, would inflict this kind of punishment, this kind of suffering, on an innocent young child. And if I had to believe that God was inflicting this kind of punishment on my son, it would have been a near impossibility of both reason and faith for me to accept. What finally emerged was the faith and recognition that God was my Father; that leukemia was an illness abroad in our world like so many other diseases; that this illness and disease was no respector of persons; and that my son, and even myself, were as vulnerable to it as anybody else. And that this God who loved me with a love that would not let me go would be with me and with my family through this experience to give grace and strength to deal with it and to bear it.

Later I was to discover that even some good could come out of it. The good would be that my faith was stronger because of this experience; the faith of my family would be stronger;

I would be able to minister to people in tragedy and suffering and in unexplainable kinds of situations in ways that I had never been able to minister before. Those are some of the good things that came out of that experience. But that experience was tragic. That experience remains tragic, and I could never put it in the category of something God wanted or willed to happen. Rather I join the doctors and medical science with all available means to fight against leukemia and all other diseases. I do not assume that disease is what God wants for humanity, but in assuming that it is a phenomenon that I cannot explain or understand, I commit myself in new dedication to seeking to eradicate that disease and others from the life of man on earth. For example, a mother whose son was hit and killed by a drunken driver does not accept that as God's will for her son, but gathers her energies and imagination and organizes Mothers Against Drunk Driving to try to eliminate as many such accidents as possible. That kind of response is a far better response than a resigned acceptance under the rubric that such an accident is "the will of God."

An important relevant point is made by Leonard Hodgson, a philosopher in the 1930s, whose insight is helpful. Though in the following quotation he is not writing about a tragic event, he approaches essentially the same question from the standpoint of one who has a narrow escape from tragedy:

> There are many stories of men who have similarly missed trains which have been wrecked, and who ascribe their eacape to Providence. If they are combining the thought of God as a celestial chess-player with the thought of God as preeminently concerned with their enjoyment of earthly life at the expense of others, there is not much to be said for their point of view. But if they are humbly acknowledging a call to further service

on earth before they pass beyond, they are rightly interpreting their escape. In all probability all the events which led up to all these men missing their various trains could be adequately accounted for in terms of the interaction of natural law, human freedom, and divine grace. But at every point within the interaction God sees what are the possibilities for good, and the man who shares His enlightment and His power and gives himself to make that good come true, has found the meaning of that moment and his 'special providence'. The gates of the future are indeed open, the universe is in the making. But only if made aright can the making stand. . . . The end is sure, for He who at every moment in the process sees its possibilities for good is God omnipotent—omnipotent to turn all circumstances to good account, to turn today's defeat into tomorrow's victory. [*Essays in Christian Philosophy* (1930), pp. 59f.]

The insight here is that events are "the interaction of natural law, human freedom, and divine grace." The other insight is that in any event God "sees what are the possibilities for good," and if the individual can share the insight of the good that God can see in any event and seek to act upon it, then it is the best response to tragic events or missed tragic events.

I am aware that some people seem to find help and gain comfort from thinking that such tragedies are the "will of God." However, there is a great risk of irreparable damage in saying to people who have experienced such tragedies that such was or is the "will of God." Another father, when told that his ill son was not going to live and when some well-meaning people indicated that his impending death was the "will of God," rejected God and never had anything to do with the Church or Christian faith thereafter. Previously he had been an extremely active churchman. Yes, in addition to it being untrue, it is dangerous to say to people whose children or who they themselves are suffering from some unexplainable tragedy that this is what God wants or is his will. Those words should never be said to such sufferers. It is more truthful and much more helpful to say, "God will not leave you in your hurt or suffering. God will be with you. God will give you strength to bear your trial. Somehow God will see you through this." This expresses a faith by which a person can survive tragedy, and I believe it is far nearer to Biblical truth.

When William Sloane Coffin, Jr., was senior Minister at the Riverside Church in New York City, his college-age son, Alex, was killed in a single-car accident. "Alex had died in the early morning of Tuesday, January 11, 1983, driving in a bad storm on a dangerous curve at the edge of South Boston Harbor. He had been in a celebratory mood that might have included a beer too many. His car had crashed through a low seawall into the water around midnight; his passenger escaped, but Alex drowned." [*William Sloane Coffin, Jr., A Holy Impatience*, by Warren Goldstein, pp. 307–308]

Two weeks later, Coffin preached a sermon entitled "Alex's Death." In it he expressed his gratitude to so many that had given him love and support. But he was angered by those who ascribed Alex's death to the will of God. "He saved his real wrath, though, for an old friend (unidentified as such) who had made the mistake of implying that Alex's death was God's will. This 'should never be said,' he told the congregation, as he described 'swarming all over her,' demanding to know if it was 'the will of God that Alex never fixed that lousy windshield wiper of his, that he was probably driving too fast in such a storm, that he probably had had a couple of frosties too many?' He confessed that 'nothing so infuriates me as the incapacity of seemingly intelligent people to get it through their heads that God doesn't go around this world with his finger on triggers, his fist around knives, his hands on steering wheels.' Quite the contrary: 'My own consolation lies in knowing that it was *not* the will of God that Alex die; that when the waves closed over the sinking car, God's heart was the first of all to break' . . . He concluded by taking the advice (and the line) from a friend's letter, promising to seek consolation 'in that love which never dies, and find peace in the dazzling grace that always is.'" [ibid., p. 310]

A young four-year-old blond-headed boy named Sammy was killed in a car accident. He was in a parking lot and a drunken driver came off the highway into the parking lot and struck the child. As the family's minister I was called and met the ambulance at the hospital. The doctors and technicians worked for several hours to save Sammy's life. My wife and I sat with the stunned parents and gave them what support we could. The doctor emerged and said, "We did everything we could, but we could not save his life." The parents were devastated. "Why? Why did this happen? Why did our Father God let this happen?" The parents were so stricken that they stayed with us at our house for three days without ever going home. Of course, we knew no answers to their or our questions of WHY. We stayed with them through their agony. But one thing that was never said or implied to them was that this was "the will of God." Who could love or trust a God who willed THAT to happen? By God's grace they finally emerged from the tragic experience, never to "get over it," but to live life beyond it by the grace of God. They were able to cling to faith in God, though they never could understand why such a tragedy would happen.

We fight against drunken driving. We fight against leukemia, and all kinds of things that harm human life. We fight against the things that happen as a result of the activity of evil people, who bring so much of "man's inhumanity to man." We fight it in the name of God because we do not believe that God wants or wills such. However, as we face the tragedy of disease or accidents or evil in our lives, we come to live with it because we must. It is the reality with which we live. We can be helped as we believe with the apostle Paul, through faith, that in everything God will be with us and by his grace give us strength to bear it and eventually learn to live beyond it. We may not see at that time how any good can come from what has happened, but it is possible that as days and weeks and months and years pass, we may be able to see that God has been at work with us to bring some good from the experience. That never includes that we come to think the tragedy itself was good. It remains a tragedy.

When Paul wrote, "We know that in everything God works for good with those who love God," he was writing out of his experience and faith with the deep conviction that God is with us in all the experiences of life including the experience of tragedy. He writes of some of the things that have happened to him: "Imprisonments, with countless beatings, and often near death. Five times I have received at the hands of the Jews the forty lashes less one. Three times I have been beaten with rods; once I was stoned. Three times I have been shipwrecked; a night and a day I have been adrift at sea; on frequent journeys, in danger from rivers, danger from robbers, danger from my own people, danger from Gentiles, danger in the city, danger in the wilderness, danger at sea, danger from false brethren; in toil and hardship, through many a sleepless night, in hunger and thirst, often without food, in cold and exposure" (2 Corinthians 11:23-28 Revised Standard Version).

If Paul had lived a life free from harsh and tragic experiences we would have reason not to believe his great affirmation. But he has been there!

The power of his great affirmation is followed by the magnificent expression of faith: "Who shall separate us from the love of Christ? Shall tribulation, or distress, or persecution, or famine, or nakedness, or peril, or sword?—No, in all these things we are more than conquerors through God who loved us. For I am sure that neither death, nor life, nor angels, nor principalities, nor things present, nor things to come, nor powers, nor height, nor depth, nor anything else in all creation, will be able to separate us from the love of God in Christ Jesus our Lord" (Romans 8:35, 37-39 Revised Standard Version).

That is pure faith! That is faith in the presence of any event of life, and it enables us to believe that ultimately no experience or tragedy has the capacity to separate us from God. God is there with us in *everything*, no matter what! That faith can help us to find our way into the sunlight of God's love and care and to a fulfilling life after tragedy, even if the "limp" from the tragedy remains.

The classic story of tragedy, loss and suffering is in the oldest book in Bible, the story of Job, the literature of both Jews and Christians. The question behind the loss of all his possessions, the sudden death of his seven sons and three daughters in a storm and the rapid deterioration of his health to the point of intense suffering, is "Why did all of this happen to the good man Job?" Why would it happen to anybody, but especially why to such a good man? The book *Why Bad Things Happen to Good People* attempts to deal with this problem, but it is still a largely unanswered question today.

When Job's three friends learned what had happened to him, they came to bring help. But unfortunately their proffered help was in the form of pat answers, and, as usually is the case when pat answers are given to deep questions, they are woefully inadequate.

At the end of the story we are left with a Job who agonizingly tried to find answers to why the horrendous events of tragedy, loss, and suffering happened to him. Through his trying experiences he clung tenaciously to faith in God.

Job's wife encouraged him to "curse God, and die" (Job 2:9 Revised Standard Version). Severe tragedy often causes the victim to want to rail out at God, shaking his or her fist at God and screaming WHY? As a deeply felt and honest expression of hurt, anger and frustration, such a temporary and normal expression is surely understood by God. However, if such a feeling and attitude becomes permanent it produces bitterness and the struggle to get beyond tragedy is lost.

Job never found satisfactory answers, but in the struggle to maintain a measure of faith he learned that he did not have to understand in order to have faith in the eternal God. And beyond all his tragedy he emerged in the sunlight of God's love to live again. The lesson Job learned hopefully can be learned by all of us who experience unexplainable tragedy. We hope also that we will be given a measure of faith in God that will enable us to get beyond tragedy and to emerge in the sunlight of God's love to live again.

*Part Two*
# CARVINGS

Thus hope carves its shape upon
the human heart.

— From "Birthday Present for Mother"

# Introduction

The "thing" crept in on silent feet. Before leaving, it became a horrible beast that was uncontrollable. In taking the life of our son, it clawed with a ferocity that tore at our faith. This book tells a part of the story of the survival of threatened spirits. It reveals the remarkable way one twelve-year-old boy handled day-by-day combat with a cruel disease.

It began on Christmas Day, 1966. Scott fainted in the sanctuary the day he united with the church. He had an operation on January 21, 1967, and it was discovered to be lymphosarcoma. Cobalt radiation followed. On March 30, 1967, his mother's birthday, the cancer reappeared in the form of leukemia. We fought this until Black Saturday, April 13, 1968, when he died. The last four months were spent in Sloan Kettering Memorial Hospital in New York.

The writings record in cameo form the writhing of the spirits of parents and two teenagers—Scott's sister and brother. They express faith and fear, hope and hurt, prayer and pain, love and loneliness. They extend over a period of a year's sorrow after Scott's death.

The title "Carvings" was suggested by a friend. It implies that the writings have been carefully cut from the large experience of suffering and grief. Our healing hearts carry hereafter the patterns of painful carvings. Revealing our inner struggles may help others who wear the many faces of illness and sorrow. Several observations by way of preface may have "underscoring" value.

We bore what did not seem possible!

God did not answer our prayers as we wanted Him to. He did not clearly answer our agonizing "whys." But He did give us sustaining grace. We know that this grace was adequate, as we looked back a year later. In the midst of it, we never knew whether we would make it.

That a son so young could teach his family so much in extended suffering seems uncanny. But from him we have learned some meaningful lessons of life. They will remain with us through whatever else is to come.

A friend experiencing a similar hurt wrote: "Strange to think, how totally personal, how unsharable, how permanent the experience is for those who live on out of it." How true that is! Some depths can never be shared. The four of us who survived are incapable of sharing all—even with each other.

But we share what we can. Perhaps God can use it to help some others in their deep hurt. It has helped me to put some of the overflow on paper

April 13, 1969
*(One year after his death.)*

# Entering a
# Strange New World

## Two at the Door

The end of the year is only hours away.
Soon a door will open—
    This one has never been opened before.
Even now I seem to hear the noise of the key,
    As it is being put in the keyhole to unlock.
I know the One who will open the door.
    He is the Lord of the years.
I cannot help but wonder what lies beyond
    The door that is being opened.

Am I afraid? Afraid is not the word.
    Interested, concerned, excited, eager,
    Anxious, pensive, anticipating,
    Uncertain, hopeful, fearful—
What would the word sound like that
    Expressed the meaning of all these?

By the knowledge of these things I am helped:
    The One who is opening the door
        Is He who has walked with me to it.
    The One who has the key
        Has told me what to call Him "Father."
    The One who opens saying, 'Walk in,"
        Will not then turn and walk away.
    The One who stands with me on the threshold
        Does not have a worried look on His face.
    The One who has the master key
        Always knows what He is doing.
    The One who turned the door knob to open

Has been both Architect and Builder.
The One—who only can be called "The One,"
This One knows my name.

And now, look. The door is opening,
A bit wider with every stroke of twelve.

December 31, 1966
*(This was written a few days before we had any knowledge
of Scott being ill.)*

## CHRISTMAS DAY

This year Christmas Day came on Sunday.
It was a special day for us.
Scott would profess publicly his faith in Jesus Christ!
He had been a part of a class of twelve-year-olds,
And together they had studied and considered
What it meant to be a Christian.
Previously, in a room alone with Scott,
I tried to say to him
What I also said to the others, one by one:
"Being a Christian is being a follower of Jesus.
Jesus is a living person and so are you.
Do you understand this and do you want to be
His follower?"
I searched his eyes and face for understanding,
Sincerity and acceptance
And I found them all there as he said,
"Yes sir, I do."
Along with all the other boys and girls
He had stood before the Session
And answered the routine questions.
He and the others had been received
Into full church membership!
In the sanctuary the people were gathered in worship.
The young people came to the baptismal font
As their names were called,
There to answer their profession questions again,
And for the baptism of those unbaptized.
(Scott had been baptized when he was a few months old.)
One by one as I called the names the youths came.

"Scott Noble," I said, and he did not come.
An elder at the font handed me a note.
"Scott fainted, but he is all right now," I read.
The strong arms of a friend had carried him out.
Two doctor friends followed them.
From one of them came the word, "He is all right now."
Little did they know, little did we know,
And least of all little did he know
That this was the beginning of the end.
In the end he would be born into another world,
The one we call Heaven.
Perhaps it was dramatically right for it to begin,
On the anniversary of our Lord's birth into this world.

May 31, 1968

## First Intimations

"What did the doctor say?"
The telephone wire carried the question
From Richmond to Anniston.
"He said the X-rays showed something there,"
Raced the words from Anniston to Richmond.
"What does this 'something there' mean, doctor?"
Words came back from the doctor,
And then the sentence that filled
The empty void with noises and shadows
Of an unknown and unshaped fear:
"Let's don't push the panic button yet."
At the moment these words were spoken,
The decision was made: Return home.

As fears mounted, faith sought to rise.
There was struggle
Not to bring tomorrow into today.
This was the beginning,

And for a long time to come
Faith and fear would be fighting each other,
And tomorrow would be surging into today.

June 12, 1968
*(I had gone to Richmond, Virginia to participate in a*
*Tower Scholarship Program at Union Theological Semi-*
*nary. My wife Betty had taken Scott for a checkup following*
*his fainting experience. I called her to find out what the*
*doctor had said concerning Scott, but without any idea that*
*there was anything seriously wrong. Her concern caused me*
*to immediately call the doctor in Anniston.)*

## Open the Door and Walk into a Strange New World

Our hearts had been filled with anxiety.
We knew the illness could be serious.
Down in the operating room the skilled surgeon worked.
Though sleeping now, the little boy had faith in him.
We waited.
The doctor came back too soon.
"I could not get it out.
It has grown on the walls . . ."
Other words were said,
But not many others were heard.
I followed him to the door
And into the corridor
To ask the question that is always asked.
He said, "Perhaps a year."
I knew he did not know,
But I feared he might be right.
Then back with his mother, I said:
"Open the door and walk into a strange new world."
With this new world we were not familiar,
But we were to learn of it.

May 29, 1968

*Standing in the Fire*

## Facing It

The doctor said to him
"We are going to have to operate
To get out what shouldn't be in your chest."
Wisely he added, "We do it all the time,
And everything will be all right."
His dark brown eyes filled to the brim,
And overflowed with a tear on each cheek.
He quickly looked at me.
I tried to conceal my hurt,
And then he slowly said, "All right."

During the night he slept so well.
There was no restlessness suggesting worry.
When morning came, he went
Without a word or a tear.
It was but the first of many evidences
Of the quality of his spirit,
And of how large a man
That had grown within him in twelve short years.

Later, much later, we talked.
"How did you feel about it?
Were you afraid?"
He said, "No, because you said the doctor
Was one of the best chest surgeons,
And because he said, 'We do it all the time,'"
Faith and trust were the warp and woof
Of the fabric of his experience.
And with him this faith and trust

46

Did not seem to come and go.
It stayed through the long difficult months.
Until faith and trust
Became sight and knowledge
At Eastertime in 1968.

And now it is a heritage he has left us,
To "walk manfully in the way of Jesus Christ"
Living in faith and trust,
Until our own Black Saturday,
And glorious Easter.

June 13, 1968
*(Two months after his death)*

## Birthday Present for Mother

From the January operation time onward
We lived and breathed anxiety.
Will it show up here?
Will it make itself known there?
Like an unknown enemy,
Under the cover of night, it lurked,
But for the time all was well.

Then came Thursday, March 30th.
"Happy Birthday, Mother. Happy Birthday."
To Atlanta! To the doctor! (always with fear)
Blood tests  Examination. The word.
Now it's in the blood!! Leukemia!!!
The distant and unfamiliar word,
Now so near.
So near it is suffocating!
Dark heavy clouds,
With just a ray of hope.
"We can do so much more now.
We believe we are getting nearer
To an answer all the time.
An answer could come in time."

Thus hope carves its shape upon the human heart.
In the meantime there is prayer and faith.
Prayer, Hurting, Faith, Hurting, Prayer, Hurting!
On and around it goes.
Always prayer! Always hurting!
The struggle always to have faith.

Somehow, God gave grace to bear
What we did not believe possible to bear.
Evil and disease gave a cruel present, and
The gift of God's daily grace was our only salvation.

June 12, 1968

## My Burden

It is a dark brown color,
Thicker at some places than at others.
But dull and heavy withal.
There are not many bright spots in it.
Occasionally there is a flicker of light
That gets to me through it.
But it is dull and heavy.
Whether it can ever be dissolved or removed,
I do not really know.

Perhaps if I could get it moved about,
So that it is not just an indescribable mass,
But carefully molded, as if by hand,
Into the shape of a cross—
Perhaps then it could be borne.

October 6, 1967

## ELOQUENT COMMUNICATION

From my secluded study,
I heard someone coming. It was Ruby.
"Do you want a cup of coffee?"
She poured it and handed it to me shakily.
"Excuse me, I am 'shakified' today," she said.
"You are too young to be 'shakified'," I said.
"Ever since I lost two sons in nine days, I get this way now and
    again."
"Two sons in nine days! How old were they?"
"One was sixteen and one was ten. They both had muscular
    dystrophy,
If you know what that is."
"Yes," I quietly answered.
But I was not thinking of the nature of the disease.
Pictures were flashing through my mind
With the speed of a drama of pathos recalled.
Two little black bodies,
The younger imitating the older,
To the deep hurt of a mother,
Who surely felt, "One was enough!"
I had seen enough of sharecropper houses
To see the small, plain rooms,
The lumpy beds and patched quilts,
But I also saw it clean and neat.
By then she was saying,
"It was on February 9th and February 18th."
(Today is February 23rd several years later.)

I think I know why she told me about it,

In a natural unpointed manner.
Only a week ago had I returned
From a month's vigil of hurt.
My son of twelve was threatened.

She could not tell me how she felt.
She could not tell me that she understood
And shared the emotions which were mine.
But the depth of her concern and feeling
She had conveyed with simple eloquence.

February 23, 1967

## She Said, "We Knelt at the Altar and Prayed For Him"

My son was sick—desperately ill!
A wonderful lady who loves and cares
Was speaking in her home of our hurt,
And of their hopes and prayers for recovery.
The maid overhead and also cared.
Perhaps she cared for the sake of her employer.
Perhaps she cared because of the costly stand
I had taken for years in behalf of her people.
Perhaps she cared because it was a child,
And she is a mother.
Perhaps she cared because
a Christian cares.


But I could see the scene,
In the small building housing "The Church of God in Christ."
Here the people struggled to raise a bit of money,
Just to do a little more "fixing" in their church.
A twenty-five dollar check was big to them.
And our church? A new building of about a million
and a quarter!
Furthermore, we were Presbyterian (and all that means),
And they were a little sect (and all that means).


And still another difference—race!
The difference of race in the very days
When our two races were in conflict.


She told them my son was sick—very sick.

The small group of them came to the altar,
With bodies tired from working for us.
Their dark faces darker yet with care and concern.
In their hearts and on their lips was the prayer:
"Lord God, you can do everything. Make his little son well."

This I believe: If God has heard
The quiet prayers of so many of us,
He has perhaps even more carefully heard
The prayers of their simple and sincere intercession.

This I know: In my hurt
I have seen the drama of brotherhood and faith!
My heart is warmed!
And I am grateful!

February 28, 1967

## Insight: He Has a Plan

During these months when the day was over,
Before going to sleep,
We would read and pray together.
One would read, another would pray as we knelt.
This night from the gospels we read
From his own red leather Bible with his name in gold.
We read of a case of healing by Jesus.
We read words about faith and prayer.
Briefly we talked of prayer and illness.
Can we ask, even in our feeble faith,
And expect God always to heal?
Is it a magic of words and faith
That always produces a magician's wonder?
Not knowing that he was really speaking of himself,
(For he felt he had gotten over his operation),
He said, "Maybe it is not in God's plan
For all to be made well."
My heart was heavy. I was afraid.
I feared this was the plan for him.
I did not want it.
Everything in me cried out,
"I believe You *can* make him well.
Help Thou my unbelief."
But I knew his insight was good:
We are in God's hands. He has a plan.

June 3, 1968

## ON HANDLING
## WHAT CANNOT BE HELPED

Perhaps there are two kinds of pain and suffering.
One is that which we bear in our own bodies.
The other is of witnessing a dearly loved one hurt.
My son experienced one kind, and I the other.
He bore his better than I bore mine,
And he taught me in the process.
In illness some pains have to be borne.
We know before the pain comes
That it is going to come,
And there is a natural recoil from it.
As he was in the throes of pain,
I tried to say that I hurt with him,
That I wish he didn't have to go through it.
With a maturity far beyond his years,
He said, "Daddy, what you can't help,
You just have to accept
And go through with it."
I said, "Yes, I know."
As I silently gave thanks for him
And his spirit under fire,
I prayed that I might handle better
My part of the suffering.

June 3, 1968

## ALWAYS FEAR AND HOPE

Up to the heights,
Down to the depths.
By some miracle he shall live!
Now we are engulfed by fear!
Fear that he shall not live.
Up and down! Always up and down.
We live almost daily with fear and hope.
With all the ups and downs,
It is no wonder that our spirits are seasick.
And there is no Dramamine that will ease it.
Yesterday it looked good and he felt well,
    And so did we.
Today it looks bad and he feels bad,
    And so do we.
Tomorrow? Nothing but big question marks.

One thing is certain: we will not give up!
Our love for him is too deep.
His eyes show that he trusts us,
And that he is counting on us.
We will hold on,
And hope for a breakthrough—a miracle.

But in the meantime—the hurt!
God! The hurt!
If we loved less,
Perhaps we would hurt less!

But in his need our love grows,
And the hurt grows.

O God, for his sake,
You have got to hold us steady.
Do not relax Your hold on us,
Because we have not the strength
To hold on to You.
"O love that will not let us go . . .
O Joy that seeks us through pain . . ."

June 8, 1968

# The School of Suffering

There were times when his pain
Was almost more than I could bear.
"I wish I could take it for you,
I hate to see children suffer,"
Were sentiments rarely expressed
But nearly always consciously felt.
One day in some intensity of suffering
They were expressed with feeling.
Can you believe the insight
That came from his weakening body,
But clear mind and courageous spirit?
"Daddy, if there were no suffering or evil here,
It would be the same as heaven.
This is just what we have to endure."
I felt as if I were learning
In the school of Christian suffering,
And there was no question
About the greatness of the spirit
Of him who was my teacher.

June 13, 1968
*(Two months after his death)*

# The Whys

## For Now, Be Careful

Don't come telling me
This is what God wants!
Don't say now that
This is His will!
Maybe the time will come
When I can hear and accept that.
But not now!
Not at the moment I see my child
Suffer from a thousand needle sticks
With hardly a complaint!
Not at the moment I see my child
Daily becoming weaker from the ravages
Of what can only be called a "cruel disease."
Not when I know how eagerly he wants to live,
And how agonizingly I want him to live.
Not when I daily feel the depth of the suffering
Of a mother's broken heart.
No, don't say it now!

Say rather, "God is with you.
He who saw His own Son suffer and die
Is with you in your Hurt."
Say, "He wants the world to be rid
Of the hate and evil that took His Son,
And He wants the world to be rid
Of the disease that takes your son."
Say, "There was unseen purpose
In His Son's death.
Could be there is unseen, but high and holy purpose

In what is now taking place."
Say, "Try to have faith and trust,
Hard though it be."
Say, "Talk to God about all your questions.
He understands the questions of a father or mother.
Do not veil them behind the cover
Of what a Christian is supposed to think or ask.
Tell Him all! Ask Him all!"

I can hear words like these.
Time will come, perhaps,
When I can say,
"We are in God's hands in life and death.
His is a wisdom higher than ours.
His is a love greater than ours.
I accept His will."
But for now, be careful,
Lest in my hurt you turn me from God.
He only is my hope and my redemption.

June 10, 1968

# WHY HIM?

Why did it come to him?
Why did it happen to us?
There are so many millions,
Why did it have to be he?
Yes, we asked this question.
And we asked a hundred others.

A magazine article says the number is 2,500.
They are the children who die
With this same disease every year.
In lands of the Orient children suffer and die,
Of varied diseases, and never see a doctor.
In Vietnam children are burned and maimed,
Incurably scarred in body and emotions,
By a cruel war, and of it they know nothing,
Except to experience the suffering and death of it.
In Africa unnumbered children silently die for the
Simple lack of food.
All over the world thousands of children grow up
Without genuine love and care.

Our child is loved!
Only God knows the measure of our love.
And God has given him the capacity to love,
For ours he has received and returned.
Spoken words of love only touched the reality
That had grown strong and rich.
And do you think that death
Could break a love like that?

Never . . .
"For I am persuaded that neither death . . ."

He was secure in a great love.
All that medical science could do
Was at his disposal.
And God was in his spirit.
He trusted. He prayed. He gave thanks.

Why him? Why us?
No, he was not singled out
And alone visited with such suffering—and death.
He is a part of a large company of sufferers.
And so are we.
But not so large a company
That God did not know his name.
God knows him—and us.
We seek to bow our heads in acceptance
And give thanks for a child of love.

June 10, 1968

# I Kept Asking Why

I kept asking why.
No answers were adequate!
They just did not make sense
To my mind and heart in suffering love.
To discipline me? Perhaps.
To touch the lives of my other children
Who might be at turning points in their lives?
    Perhaps.
The list of good things that God might
Do through it,
Could be extended on and on.
But my hurting heart and mind
Steadfastly refused to accept the fact
That any or all of these things
Were big enough to warrant
Cutting off the life of this one
Whose promise cast so clear a shape!

In the hotel room I could not sleep.
I lay awake listening to sounds of city night,
But most of all examining every
Shape, form, size and color of "why."
Then something came.
If God has something else for him,
Something that is bigger, more wonderful,
Something that He wants him to do now,
When he is at the earthly age of thirteen,
Then it would be justifiable for him to go.
But only something so great and big

That it would justify taking him now,
Would even come near answering
The questions of my searching and agonizing mind.

And this I believe.
God, who is able to do such wonders
With human life here,
Can surely plan for and do even greater wonders
With human life in heaven's world.
God must have had some purpose for him,
Big enough to make it be "Fatherly God" right,
For him to say through the door of such an illness,
"Come, Scott, I have something for you to do here."
And Scott said, "Yes Sir!"

June 7, 1968

## The Big "Why?"

Why do little children suffer?
Perhaps of all questions this is the hardest.
   The little ones of Vietnam,
   Who do not know the meaning of the conflict,
   But who know it all too well.
   The little ones who have neither bread nor heat
   And without blame suffer inside and out.
   The little ones who are dreadfully sick
   Who cry out in hurt and pain.
   The little ones just old enough to know enough
   To endure heroically, and to fight back manfully.
For adults who have shared in sin,
And here and there have failed to do
What they should have done,
And who perhaps each one carries within himself
Some reason for blame or punishment—
For them to suffer is to some degree understandable.
But why? Why, God, should wonderful, little,
Innocent, helpless children suffer?
Why?
Let one who has stood beside
His own dear child and daily
Watched him endure in his body
Pain and suffering—

Let such a one talk, and
I will try to listen.
But, please, no glib answer from one
Who has not entered a child's suffering.
    Perhaps for me, this is the largest of questions.
    Perhaps only God can answer this question,
    Because perhaps only God knows.

        February to April, 1968
        *(In New York City)*

# Lord, I Believe—Help My Unbelief!

During the long days of his illness,
Perhaps one prayer was repeated
Time without number:
"Lord, I believe! Help my unbelief!"
Deep down I believed God could heal my son.
But I told myself that God might not.
Should I have committed myself emotionally
And every other way to the proposition
That God would heal him?
Is that what faith means?
This is what I yearned to do,
But was it sound and right?
Did not Jesus pray, "Father, remove this cup."
And then more.
Should He have committed Himself
To the proposition that God
Was going to remove the cup?
Obviously there was something higher here.

With all my heart I wanted to believe
That God was going to make him well.
I entreated Him to do it, not three times,
But a thousand, thousand times.
I cannot believe that my son and I
Had to drink together the cup of suffering and death,
Because I could not mentally and emotionally say,
"I have prayed. God is going to make him well,
     And that is it."
But I didn't want any lack of faith in my heart,

Because faith is strong and effective—
And so I prayed:
"Lord, I believe! Help my unbelief!"

And now it is done.
The cup was not removed.
We drank its dregs.
Crucifixion was in His plan.
Burial followed.
But God is not through.
Crucifixion, death, and burial are not the end.
There is yet resurrection and life—always life.

And still I pray:
"Lord, I believe. Help my unbelief.
Through it all I still have faith.
Enlarge my faith and my belief.
Shrink my doubt and unbelief."

June 21, 1968

# The Darkest Deep

# To Die

To die.
What is it to die?
I want to be born into a life
Where there is no death,
No suffering, and there are no limitations.
Then when God gives this birth, called death,
To my loved one before He does to me,
Shall I be engulfed in selfish despair?
I trust not.
I pray not.

October 6, 1967

# THE ONLY WAY IS THROUGH IT

Make no mistake about it—it is a big thing!
His human life is ended—it is all over,
And we have been left with a big sorrow.
We are as much face to face with it as we can get,
And it is not an experience to be desired.
But there is no way around it!
Furthermore, there is no way over or under it.
The only way is through it.
And we shall get through it.
We shall never be the same again,
(And that is not all bad),
But we shall get through it.
And this is our faith:
God goes through it with us.

May 29, 1968

## SURVIVAL BY GRACE

In Peru a whole town disappeared
When a volcano erupted
And molten lava engulfed
The people without warning..

Tragedy sometimes comes without warning.
Then how does one survive?
Perhaps it takes a miracle of God,
And could this be the meaning of grace?

## THEY TOOK IT WITH CHRISTIAN TOUGHNESS

It was near Christmastime,
And the problem was intensifying for our family.
We had gone through most of the drugs,
And not many were left.
There remained one big hope—
*Time* magazine's articles about L-asparaginase.
If they would take us, we would go to New York.

I can see them now as I told them,
In more frank and open detail than ever before:
"This just might work!
Could be they have found the answer!
But if not, then . . . this is it."

How hurt they were!
But with what strong toughness they took it.
We cited examples of faith and courage
That was a part of their heritage
From both sides of their family.
"The blood from both is in your veins,
And God will help you with this hurt."

Through four long months,
They lived with it as we did,
Except theirs might have been the harder part.

They were each away in school
And had to handle it alone!

There were the Christmas holidays
And the spring holidays,
And one other time when they came to New York,
But other than that—it was theirs to handle.

And handle it they did!
When spring holidays ended,
They each walked into his room
(And they knew all too well)
To talk to him one last time.
We stood in the corridor,
Because this was theirs.
What happened and what was said
Is theirs alone—as it should be.

Our family knew a verse:
"Trust in the Lord with all your heart,
And lean not unto your own understanding."
There was no understanding of this,
And perhaps all that was left was trust.

It is no wonder that we had it engraved
In stone where his body lies.
Perhaps it is engraved even more permanently
In four minds, and hearts, and lives.

April 9, 1969

# *Dawn*

# He Did Not Miss Easter

Days almost lose their names and numbers,
After nearly four months in the hospital.
"What is today?" he asked.
"Sunday. Palm Sunday," we replied.
Almost in surprise, he said, "Next Sunday is Easter!
Aw! I've missed it too."
He wanted to be able to go home.
He had missed Christmas at home.
He had missed school in the winter and spring.
And now he felt he had missed Easter too.

But Easter is one thing he did not miss!
When in the early dawn of Black Saturday,
He took his last quiet breath,
Easter was his, and his forever.
Now he knew, far better than we,
The meaning of the words,
"Today Thou shalt be with me in Paradise."

He did miss some things,
But Easter was not one of them.

July 10, 1968

# I Sat in the Pew on Easter Sunday

I went to Church on Easter Sunday,
But this Easter I sat in the pew.
It was the only light I had
From death on Black Saturday,
To burial on Easter Monday.

I heard the words of resurrection Scripture,
I sang the notes of resurrection hymns.
I felt the triumphant strains from the organ.
I heard the minister's words of resurrection faith.
I looked at the cross of suffering,
Which had been embedded in my heart for over a year.
I saw the table with its word of life,
Which word had been my yearning for over a year.
I fixed my eyes on the symbol of the crown.
It was rich in color, and the light through it
Cast its luster on everything.
And I knew the crown meant
"Eternal Life," "Victory," "Lordship," and "Reward,"
And I worshiped.

I suppose I have always believed in resurrection.
I do not know a time when I haven't.
But now to say that I believe in resurrection,
Is not adequate.

Resurrection is my food and my drink.
It is the breath I inhale and exhale.
It is the shape of my soul.
It is my life.

July 10, 1968

## DEATH'S TWO SIDES

There are some hard tough facts of life,
And death is one of them.
When it comes, it is real through and through.
Hearts may break,
Tears may flow,
Spirits may suffer,
But when death comes to a loved one,
It has come!
It has come with all its earthly finality.
Longing, yearning, seeking, praying—
Nothing will change the irrevocable fact.

But that is only one side of death.
It is the side from which we enter death,
And it is on this side that we stand
As we experience the death of our loved one.
But death has another side,
Just as real as this side.
It is the resurrection side!
It is the eternal life side!
From death our loved one emerges
With the thrilling excitement of fullness of life.
Now he lives!
Now he sees face to face!

Now he knows even as he is known!
Now there is fullness of Joy forevermore!

Hard tough facts of life?

Don't stop when you tell me
That death is a hard tough fact.
I know it is.
But this I also know:
Life is tougher than death!
In the presence of life that God gives,
Death must move aside.
Death has its limits
And has now done its worst.
Life, eternal life, has taken over!
And when I see him
(A hundred times a day!)
He is pulsating with the joy of life!
Thanks be unto Jesus Christ our Lord.

June 10, 1968

# Homecoming

We had been gone several months,
But now we were winging our way home.
Gently the plane touched down,
And nosed in to the terminal.
Out came the passengers one by one.
Not by choice but by circumstances,
We were delayed as many went before us.
A small crowd was waiting,
Greeting loved ones and friends,
One by one as they emerged.
Then our moment came.
A brown, touseled head,
Searching, eager eyes,
And then a joyous smile,
And the happy words on his lips,
"Mother." "Daddy."

How long the delay will be,
I do not know.
But the moment will come
When the plane shall gently touch down,
And I shall step out

At the port in eternity—
And this I know:
I shall see a touseled head,
Searching, eager eyes,
A joyous smile,
And hear him say, "At last and forever!"

June 8, 1968

# Aftermath

## The Loneliness Is There

The loneliness is there.
Even if people are everywhere,
The loneliness is there.
It comes flooding in at night,
As if to engulf and overwhelm,
No matter how bravely the spirit tries.
His face—the many expressions
That have played upon it.
Joy! Happiness! Thrill! Excitement!
The warmth of love! His trust!
How I long to see his face.
His voice. "Daddy." "Mother."
His deep, almost uncontrollable laugh.
His ear. His hand. His hair.
His walk with a spring.

We have only the pictures.
Some are in the drawers,
Others are out for all to see.
But still others, hundreds of others
Until death will be in my mind and heart.

June 8, 1968

# There Is One Mercy

There is one mercy in this kind of illness.
We did not cause it.
We are left with a load of hurt and sorrow,
But we do not have the added burden of guilt.

We discovered it.
There it was: hard and horrible.
The best skills of medical science were used.
The best care a parent's love could offer was given.
The earnest prayers of a yearning family,
Enlarged literally by unnumbered Christians,
Were offered before His eternal throne.
"Let him live! If you will, let him live!"
But it was not to be.
For reasons unknown to us
He was to be the first of us
Born to new life beyond the gate of death.

Free from the guilt of
"Why did we?" or "Why didn't we?"
Our wounded spirit and broken hearts will heal.
The wound is deep, but it is clean.

July 25, 1968

# His Happy Years

Fellow sufferers were his friends.
He talked to boys from the North and West.
Football and baseball, but always football!
Scouts and camping,
Family picnics and outings,
Hunting and dogs,
Vacations and water skiing.
School and friends.
His twelve years had been so full,
And they had been happy sunny years.
Now his topics of conversation
Were but the overflow of good times.
Perhaps, as he had so much to share with others,
He realized in comparison how much he had done
And the happiness that had been his.
From his bed (his final bed)
He talked of what he wanted yet to do,
And added, with the joy of youth,
"I have already had such happy years!"
And he had!
How grateful we are for every happy year.

> June 13, 1968
> *(Two months after his death)*

## WE HAVE THIS HERITAGE

He has left us a lot.
The coin collection with the evidence
Of hours of time he spent on it.
The Hardy Boys series,
Most of which he had read.
Models put together, games he had played,
Mementoes he had saved.
And there was a scrapbook he had made.
A yellow football helmet with black stripes,
And a baseball glove.
The football we had passed and kicked,
And the baseball we had pitched and hit.
There was the wonderful autographed football!
Everything was so neatly placed in his room.
Even here his orderliness and discipline were evident.

We have his permanent school record,
With his superior ratings,
And his six-and-one-half years
Of almost solid display of A's.
There were just enough B's in the right places.
Two in conduct! (Talked too much! So full of life.)

We do have a lot of things
But that is not really what he left us.

What he left us is imperishable.
He left us the heritage of a spirit
That had matured beyond its years.

A simple but deep faith in God,
A habit of Bible reading and prayer,
A gentleness to less fortunate children,
An ability to handle disappointment,
An inner discipline of mind and spirit,
A fair, competitive spirit that kept him trying,
And a strong will to win.

And the revelations of the last year:
    A spirit with
        Courage without place for cowardice,
        Stamina without a thought of giving up,
        Manliness in the presence of pain,
        Faith in the presence of questions,
        Patience in extended suffering,
        Humor for a touch of lightness,
        And love—always wholesome love!
        For parents, for brother and sister,
        And all those about him.
We have this heritage—and so much more!

July 18, 1968

# We Are Not in Charge

We are not in charge.
We are not in charge of life.
We are not in charge of much about life.
O, we can do many things,
And we are responsible for many things.
But, in the final analysis,
We are not really in charge.

If so, I would never say,
"Let him go at thirteen!"
If so, I would never say,
"Let such suffering come upon him!"

But I do not mean to accuse God.
Life is set up in such a manner
That suffering and death are in its pattern.
We have the capacity to bring on suffering,
And even death!
We have the ability to help ease suffering,
And even to hold back death (for a time).
But there are limits to what we can do . . .
Concerning all ultimates
And many not so ultimates,
We are not really in charge!

What does one do who does not believe in God?
How does one live who does not believe in God?
If not God, who or what is in charge?
Are we but living on the top of a table,

Upon which a little light is shining,
While all around there is nothing
But the dark unknown,
Out of which there comes
The unexplainable blasts of wind
Or the cruel blows of a whip?
If I so believe,
It is no wonder I am a cynic.
It is no wonder life has no meaning.
It is no wonder I am filled
With a strange mixture of "I don't care" and fear.

I am not in charge of much,
And about me there is much darkness.
But for me to live I must believe
Someone is there.
The One who is there is wiser than I
And Jesus said He knows my name and loves me.
In this faith, I can live.

July 10, 1968

# New Life—With a Limp and a Sacrament

## There Are Some Hard
## and Tough Things in Life

There are some hard and tough things in life.
Perhaps it is a wonder there are not more people
Who tear apart in face of them.

There are so many jagged edges,
So many rusty nails sticking up,
So many broken planks
Hanging at head level,
So many loose bricks
That may fall at any minute.
Even by being careful
One does not miss all the rough spots
And if one spends all his time
And all his energy in trying to be careful,
What else can he do?

When God made man and woman,
He created the human spirit
In His own image.
Could be this is why humans too are tough.
Perhaps people expect to be hurt.
And perhaps they expect also
To go on doing their God-given task.
At least it is a fact that we get hurt.
It is also a fact that many tough spirits

Do not sit around just nursing their hurts.
But by something that God has put in us,
Or gives us when we have been hurt,
We go on to our work,
Usually with new and deeper feeling,
And sometimes with a limp.

July 10, 1968

## WHOLESOME INNER DISCIPLINE

I need a wholesome inner discipline.
One that enables me to say "no"
To diversions that would derail me.
One that causes me to stick to this now
In order that I may do the other later.
One that gives me ability to sacrifice
The small gain of the present,
For the larger gain of the future.
One that leaves me in control of my spirit
When I am faced with difficulty or pain.
One that keeps me going toward
The higher and better purposes
That my faith has set for me.

I need an inner discipline
That does not make me tense and rigid,
Nor brittle under the uncontrollable changes,
But one with sufficient resiliency
So that little failures do not break me.

I have a clearer sense of the meaning of wholesome
Inner discipline, because I saw it in his young life.

July 24, 1968

# There Is a New Shape to Life

Slowly healing will come,
But even when it comes
The scar will always be there.
And at times it will feel
As if the wound is new and fresh.
Poignant memories
And a blessing and a pain.
Scenes from earlier years,
And from later days
Come again and again
To bring a strange mixture
Of joy and pain.

In my heart and life
There has come a new dimension.
For one thing, there is a stronger desire
For integrity, honor, purpose, and meaning.
There is more craving
For the clean, the pure, and the wholesome.
Things matter, but not as much.
I knew that Paul said,
    "Whatever is honorable
    Whatever is pure,
    Whatever is lovely,
    Whatever is gracious...
Think about these things,"
But now it is more natural to do so.

I cannot quite define it

Or describe it.
But there is a new shape to life,
And it can never fit altogether comfortably
In the old forms and patterns.

July 24, 1968

# One Year Later

Last year there was no spring.
The flowers came up and bloomed,
And the trees budded and leafed out.
But last year there was no spring for us.
    Our flowers had been cut before they bloomed.
    Our trees had been severely hacked back to the trunks.

But once again there is spring.
The flowers are blooming,
And the trees are budding.
And miracle!
There seems to be spring for us too.
    Life has seeped back into our beings,
    And we are beginning to know the joy of living again.

It is the resurrection season,
And we are confident that he is living.
It is the resurrection season,
And we are beginning to be resurrected too.
And how wonderful is the resurgence of new life.

We shall not be as we were before,
For there is an added dimension
And a new depth to this new life.
The new life has grown around last year's hurt,

And has not removed it or obscured it,
But has made of it a sacrament.
And it shall remain a sacrament through the years.

March 27, 1969

*Part Three*
# FAMILY REFLECTIONS

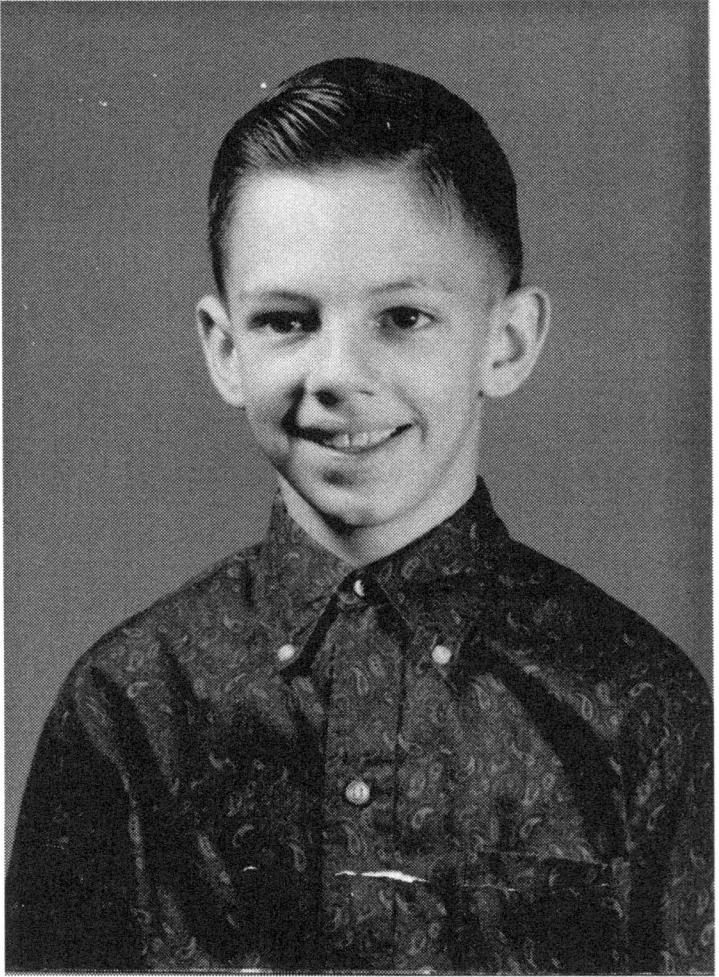

MILTON SCOTT NOBLE
*1963, nine years old*

# A MOTHER'S REFLECTION

A mother's love for her child is deep beyond the ability to understand. In like manner the mother's hurt in the loss of a child is deep beyond understanding. I have often said, "A mother never stops being a mother." The love and concern is always there.

A mother carries her child for nine months. She rejoices when the child is born and is grateful to see that her child has five fingers on each hand and five toes on each foot. She looks into the two new eyes and savors the first moment of seeing her child. So little! So fragile! So wonderful! A miracle of birth! A new life! She will always be a mother to this child no matter if he or she lives long and grows old. A mother never stops being a mother.

She cuddles the baby to her breast. She watches as he sleeps. She hears his awakening cry. She strokes the softness of his skin. She notices the first time he is able to turn over. She puts a rattle in his hands. Every coo warms the love she already feels. She marks his first step. She thrills at his first word. It is probably some form of the word "mama." She watches him grow. She is anxious when he is sick, even with a cold. She cuddles him when he falls and hurts his knee. She carefully gets him ready for his first day of kindergarten or school. He has begun. She ponders. How will he do in school? What will he grow up to be? Bit by bit she teaches him some lessons of life. She wants him to be a good strong person with character, a big heart and a good mind. If necessary she is willing to make sacrifices for him. She swells with pride when he does well in school. She worries when he does not do well. If anybody mistreats her child they will have to deal with her.

This is but the tip of her love. It is what shows, but underneath there is a big and deep love that cannot be described.

So Scott was my third child. I felt and did all of the above. Scott was smart and happy and a quick wited child. He was greatly loved by his sister and brother. Phil and I enjoyed him and had learned to relax about him as parents often do after their first children. We were so blessed; three promising children, growing, smart and healthy.

Then came Christmas in 1966. Scott fainted in Church. Nothing serious, we thought. But it probably needed to be checked out. Early January, Phil was at a meeting at Union Theological Seminary in Richmond, Virginia. I took Scott to the doctor. X-rays were taken of his chest, and something was there. The doctors, who were friends, tried to minimize what might be the problem. Phil called the doctor from Richmond and came home immediately. Further x-rays and examination clearly showed what might be a big problem. This was in his chest, and my relative in Jackson, Mississippi, Dr. James Hardy, was a heart specialist who had done one of the first heart transplants.

I wanted us to take Scott to him. An operation was indicated. When Jim came out of the operating room, he quietly said, "I could not get it all." I had been filled with anxiety but this was a cruel blow that went far beyond anxiety. How could I bear it? But there was hope. Radiation might remove it.

I had known about Emory University Hospital and Clinic all my life, and understood that it was a good facility. I wanted the best possible for Scott and I felt he could get good radiation treatment there. From the last couple of weeks in January and through March he was given radiation every week, sometimes twice a week. Phil and I usually took him for his treatment. However, for some reason, on March 30th, my birthday, I did not go with Phil and Scott. When they returned Phil told me that Scott's situation had gone into leukemia. At this time almost nobody survived leukemia. The news was an absolutely crushing blow.

Without going into more details we fought against and struggled with leukemia until April the following year, where he died in Sloan-Kettering Hospital in New York. He had been there for four months in an experimental program where there was hope that a breakthrough had been found to cure leukemia. It was not to be.

We survived with faith and trust in God, but never understanding why it happened. My family's Bible verse, "Trust in the Lord with all thy heart, and lean not unto thine own understanding. In all thy ways acknowledge him, and he will direct your paths," was my anchor. I said it over and over again and again. The strong faith of my family that I grew up in gave me support. My minister husband, Phil, said that Job in the Bible through all his suffering and loss learned that one does not have to understand to have faith. I certainly did not understand, and I tried to have faith.

I gradually experienced the lessening of pain and hurt, but deep down it is still there after all the years that have passed. But I think this experience of Scott's suffering and death made me probe more deeply into the meaning of life. It has made me a more caring person than I might have been.

The following years have been good. We are blessed in numerous ways and are filled with gratitude as we move into our older years.

# From Scott's Sister

When my father asked me to write a piece entitled "Reflections from Scott's Sister" to accompany his book, I felt honored. I thought: "What a good idea to have my brother and I to do such reflection pieces!" Being quite a methodical person, I told my father I wanted to read what he had written up to this point so that what I said would flow from, fit with, and connect with the rest of the book. I planned to read through the sections of the book, jot down my reactions, comments, and ideas as they popped into my head, make an outline from those ideas, and then write and revise the piece. I set aside Sunday mornings before church to work on this task. After all, that was how I had written other papers in my life; and during seven years of graduate school, I had written many other papers, mainly research papers, including a dissertation that I had worked on for *many* years. I thought I could write about the impact the experience had for me personally and professionally. I imagined it might take a month or six weeks to finish. How naive I was to think that I could use the approach I'd learned in my advanced placement English class and my doctoral program in psychology to reflect on the death of my brother.

As I spent Sunday mornings rereading the poems—I'd read them years before—and the sermon "Tragedy and the Will of God," I found myself overcome with tears each time. What were those tears about? I don't know. It had been thirty-six years since Scott died. Maybe a mixture of my own sorrow—yes. A reliving of the experience—yes, partially. The realization of what we had all lived through—yes. All I know is I remember telling my brother Phillip: "When you work on this, be sure you are by yourself and have privacy because it's a gut-wrenching experience." I think more than anything what was hard was the immense pain that spoke to me as I read the poems Daddy had written. The pain leapt up from the pages and engulfed me. And these were not just the words of any father; these were the words of my father. My father that I love so dearly and respect beyond measure.

Sure Scott's death was painful and hard for all of us and each experienced it in his/her own way. But the pain and suffering that leapt up at me from those pages was so real and so deep, that I found myself many Sunday mornings sitting with the manuscript in a daze, crying—not out-loud, can't-catch-your-breath sobs—but the quiet tears that roll down your cheeks and drip on the paper, the tears that come from way down deep, the tears of feeling what you know in your head, the tears of realizing what indescribable pain my father and mother went through. Although we have talked about Scott over the years and continue to do so, I've always had the sense that we shouldn't talk about Scott too much because it was too painful for Daddy. This has been somewhat frustrating for me because I always wanted to talk more about Scott. After rereading the poems I have a greater realization of my father's enormous loss.

Mary Catherine White, Daddy's secretary at the church in Anniston for fifteen years and a close family friend, said to me on several occasions: "How your Daddy walked up in that pulpit and said the words he did the first time he preached after Scott died I'll never know." Apparently he preached a sermon entitled "Resurrection Meditation" about the reality of resurrection of Jesus and also for us. Beyond being confronted by death, we are confronted with the reality of life beyond death. The sermon was followed by Communion of the Lord's Supper from the beautiful marble table upon which was carved the words, "I am the Life." The depth of faith he demonstrated in preaching that sermon as well as the one that is in this book is such an inspiration to me. Because of my immense love and overwhelming respect for my dear, dear father and to honor the memory of my brother, Scott, who gave me such a legacy, I'm attempting to get beyond the tears to write about the experience—abandoning the notes, the structure, the organization, and—as Daddy says—just writing from the heart.

I remember when Daddy told me that Scott had leukemia. It was spring of my senior year in high school, and I was working on a research paper for an advanced placement (AP) English class. In retrospect, how ironic was the topic of the paper and the specific book I was reading then. Scott had fainted in church just before Christmas, the day he was being confirmed as a member of the Church along with his friends in the Church Membership Class. Soon thereafter he had surgery in Jackson, Mississippi, to remove a tumor between his heart and his lungs. My mother had wanted Dr. James Hardy to do the operation. Hardy, a skilled surgeon who pioneered in heart transplants, was the husband of her first cousin Louise (Weesie) Sams, her best buddy growing up. (I've heard for years story after story about their adventures at "the barn" with Oscar, the old black man who officially took care of the horses and unofficially took care of the children. The barn was behind 312 South Candler, the house that Colonel George Washington Scott, the founder of Agnes Scott College, built for his son George Bucher Scott, my mother's grandfather.)

I had been staying with Mrs. White while my parents were with Scott in Jackson. I remember thinking when I saw them at the airport as they came back from Mississippi how very much they seemed to have aged since I'd seen them last.

I don't remember all the details of the paper for the AP English class. We had been asked to select a topic, research it by reading novels, and then write a paper. It was the biggest and longest paper I'd ever done. The topic I'd chosen was something about people who were in difficult situations that were beyond their control and how they cope with the situations. I can't remember all the books but I remember one was by Somerset Maugham about a man who had a clubfoot, one was about Helen Keller, and another was the *Diary of Anne Frank*. The book I was reading when Daddy told me about Scott was *Death Be Not Proud* by John Gunther. It was about a boy (sixteen, I think) who was dying or who had died from a brain tumor . . . I don't remember the exact details. I was in my bedroom reading this book and Daddy came in my room and told me about Scott. I don't remember his exact words or phrases. You'd think I'd remember such significant words. But I have a clear picture in my mind of seeing Daddy walk down the steps after he'd told me, feeling stunned and thinking how ironic that I was reading this particular book at this time. I remember feeling afraid that Scott would die like the boy in the book. And in about a year he did.

Some of my memories of Scott's last year are very clear and some are quite vague. Now I wish I could remember *everything* about him! But I was just living my life, doing the things that children do as they grow up, involved in lots of activities and enjoying my friends. I wasn't aware that my brother was going to die and I wasn't always thinking I need to remember this! But many memories stand out from earlier years. I remember Scott as a well-rounded boy who had many interests and activities. He was very smart and did well in school though I don't remember that he spent a lot of time studying. But none of us really did. We were not like the children I see today who go to elite schools and start life's pressure-cooker early on. We went to the public Woodstock Elementary school, as did all of my friends. There were no private schools in Anniston in those days. The school was a half a block from my house and we enjoyed its playground and ball fields.

Scott was in the sixth grade when he got sick. His teacher that year was Mrs. Joy Dark. She went to our church. She was a rather young teacher and my memory is that Scott liked her a lot. The year before, a church member had arranged for Daddy to spend the spring and summer studying in Edinburgh, Scotland. While he was there, he had ordered a kilt for Scott, who was so excited about getting it and had told his classmates all about it. They were excited too and anticipated the arrival of the kilt. The class must have talked about kilts and how they were different from boys' pants, more like skirts. When the long-awaited package came, one of the boys went running into Scott's class and excitedly exclaimed, "Mrs. Dark, Mrs. Dark! Scott's dress done come!" I don't think Scott ever wore the kilt. He must have been too embarrassed after that.

I have more memories of Scott being involved in Little League baseball and football. I can picture him now in his uniforms. He was the quarterback of his football team. One year, he was quarterback of the city all-star team. I have memories of a "Toys for Tots" ballgame in the late fall at the high school football field, probably the fall before he fainted in church in December. Every time I see the words "Toys for Tots" I think of Scott and that game.

I have other memories of him in his bedroom sitting at a card table, building models of cars and rockets and going over his coin collection. I remember him going to the local bookstore several blocks away and talking with the owner about his coin collection and trading coins. We still have a few pieces of his coin collection framed along with his Boy Scout medals. He also was involved in Boy Scouts and I remember him working to earn merit badges and the God and Country Scout Award. He went to scout camp at Camp Comer in Mentone, Alabama, including the summer after he was sick. The Scott Noble Memorial Chapel, built with gifts in memory of Scott, is a very special place. It's in a beautiful wooded setting that looks out over the water. My imagining and hope is that some scouts have had meaningful, thoughtful, quiet moments there.

I remember a time our family was on a picnic. We liked to walk in the woods and picnic on Sunday afternoons. Scott was really little, about three or four. I think we had just moved to Anniston. Daddy was taking pictures and Scott cried because he didn't want his picture taken. We have slides of that picnic and of Scott crying. We also had an old collie named Bonnie that a family in the church had given us because they were moving away and couldn't take the dog. I remember all three of us using Bonnie as a pillow while lying on the floor watching television, although most of the time we were outside playing or involved in activities.

I remember another dog named Wendy, who used to follow

Scott around everywhere when he was sick. Anniston was a rather small town and we could walk all over the neighborhoods to our activities and to see our friends. I have memories of Scott walking to the YMCA with Wendy, and Wendy curling up underneath the pool table while Scott played. A YMCA employee later told me pets weren't allowed, but he let Wendy in. Wendy ran away and never returned the year Scott was in the hospital in New York.

Some of Scott's special friends were Norman Thomas, Terry Braxton, Mark Landers, and Morris Culberson. I also remember a time, a year or two before Scott got sick, when he had a girlfriend named Lucy Mayne. Either Phillip or I painted on the playhouse next to our garage, "Scott Noble + Lucy Mayne" or "Scott Noble loves Lucy Mayne." Scott got really upset and Mother made us paint over it. The playhouse and garage were right next to the alleys that ran behind the houses in some Anniston neighborhoods. People put their trash cans along these alleys. I remember Scott being so excited when the workers came on the big trucks to haul the garbage away. He told Mother he wanted to be a "Gobbage-Man" when he grew up.

Scott was very sweet, quite funny, and extremely verbal. I have memories of him telling us stories at mealtimes, especially supper—funny things that happened at school, with his friends, and with his activities. He'd tell this story/poem about "The Old Lady Who Swallowed a Fly." The way he told it was so funny we'd all die laughing, and he would tell it to us over and over again. He was a picky eater so I guess he talked and told stories instead of eating. He would tease Daddy if he messed up in church. I remember him saying "Great going, Big Reverend," if Daddy had made a mistake in his sermon. Mother says he used to say: "Daddy got on a long road" when we were going on a trip, and it seemed like we were never going to get there. I also remember peeling apples for him because he didn't like the skin. Once I remember him hiding under my bed and jumping out and scaring me as I was singing along with the radio. On the radio was a popular song, an Elvis Presley song, "Suspicion." I was singing and trying to dance in front of the mirror. He jumped out from under my bed, sang a few words with me, and we laughed and laughed.

He liked to read, and I remember him reading the Hardy Boys as well as the Landmark biography series. He started taking piano at some point, and I found some of his sheet music with his name on it in the same box with his baseball glove. Also, I remember him writing a humorous story during my senior year in high school about me running away with my previous boyfriend, Moses, who'd gone to St. Bernard's College, to get married, and coming back to get my petti pants (like half slips you'd wear under your culottes). The date on the story is December 26, 1966, the day after he fainted in church.

Betty and Moses

Betty and Moses were deeply in love. So one day they ran off together to [Australia]. Betty said, "It's cold down here, Moses, and I forgot my Petti Pants." So they went back to Betty's house to get her Petti Pants. Betty said, "There's a window by the top of this tree I can climb in. I can get them and climb down the tree and nobody will ever know." But when Betty was climbing in the window, she stepped on Phillip's head. "Ow." Mumbled Phillip and woke up. "Be quiet." Said Betty. "I'll give you a cigarette if you won't tell Daddy I came." "Okay, but you're getting [gypped]," said Phillip. Betty got her Petti Pants, told Phillip where they were going and left.

The Rev.'s birddogs were howling that night and made Scott wake up. Scott told the Rev. that he heard Betty and Phillip talking. "Where did Betty go?" demanded the Rev. "I can't tell you," said Phillip. "You'd better, or I'll make you read five chapters from the Bible." Said the Rev. "Okay, I'll write it down on a piece of paper." Said Phillip. Now Phillip who can't spell worth a flip, wrote AUSTRIA instead of [AUSTRALIA]. So the Rev. took the church's money and went to Austria to look for Betty. After he had looked all over Austria, and couldn't find her, he came back. "She wasn't there," said the Rev. "Maybe he meant Australia," said Popesy. "That's what I wrote," said Phillip, "Australia, A-U-S-T-R-I-A." That's Austria you jack!" said the Rev. "Watch your language, Phil." Said Popesy. So the Rev. borrowed some money from Scott and started to go to Australia. But on the plane, the Rev. saw Betty and Moses. "You can have her back, Rev. Noble. She wears out too many pairs of Petti Pants, and every night her side sinks in so much, I roll off the bed." So Moses went back to St. Bernard, Betty went back to Nan and her horse, and the Rev. went back to his preaching.

The End

Author: Scott Noble

Scott's reference to my horse and Nan, my best friend at that time, was because I had a horse named Czar that was kept in her pasture. I had many happy days riding horses and camping out in the pasture. I'm so glad Mother saved this story for me. Scott captures well some of the family idiosyncrasies. I'll always treasure it as well as any memory of Scott I have. I am struck that it was written just about the time Scott's illness was emerging.

Strangely, my memories of his last year are less clear. Maybe they are repressed. Maybe I have transformed them naturally. I don't know. Just over a year passed from when they came home from Mississippi after Scott's surgery and when Scott died. It was the end of my senior year in high school and my freshman year at Agnes Scott. I remember a wonderful picture of Scott that Daddy had made [see page 16] for Mother's Day or as a late birthday present for Mother (her birthday is March 30th, the day she found out Scott had leukemia). It's such a very good picture of him before he started showing the signs of his treatments. Scott was rather slim but when he took Prednisone [a steroid treatment for the immune system], it made him gain weight and he lost some of his hair. I have a mental image of his round face and thinning hair. He continued to play ball that spring and summer and I can picture him in a baseball uniform with his round cheeks.

I don't remember much about my high school graduation. I remember walking across the stage behind Arthur Murray, my AP English teacher's son (I had been on the swim team as a child with him and his brother was Scott's age). We were singing or humming the song, "Ain't too Proud to Beg." Daddy preached the baccalaureate sermon on May 28, 1967. Nan Woodruff, my best friend at that time in high school, said Daddy spoke on the topic "Dreams are just dreams unless they are with God."

That summer I worked at Wakefield's clothing store in the ladies' department and I spent a good bit of time getting ready for college. Back then we had to wear dresses to class, and it mattered what you looked like. (I remember my dear sweet mother helping me get my clothes ready so that I'd "look right" for my first year at Agnes Scott. How ironic that was, given that my last year of college, about all I wore were old T-shirts and overalls from horseback riding days.) At the end of the summer we went on vacation for a week to Lake Jackson in Georgia. My aunt and uncle had a lake house there with a boat. We were going to ski! I had been once before and loved it! I guess Mother and Daddy knew this would probably be our last vacation together; maybe we all did on some level. One memory stands out. Scott had been skiing and had fallen, and Daddy was driving the boat around to pick him up. Somehow the boat ran over Scott, and Daddy froze. I was sitting at the front of the boat with him and said: "Cut off the motor!" Then Scott popped up on the other side of the boat laughing and saying something like "Well, run over me one time, Big Reverend!" We enjoyed that time together as a family. The song "Sitting on the Dock of the Bay" was popular then and I remember spending some time just doing that, wondering what was going to happen to Scott and to all of us.

The first day of college came and went, and I guess I "looked right." My grandparents Nanny and Papa lived only a block or so from Agnes Scott. I remember that fall seeing Scott and Mother and Daddy at Emory Hospital when Scott would come for his treatments. Sometime that fall Daddy and Scott went hunting because there is a picture of Scott with a deer. In the picture, Scott has round cheeks and wears hunting clothes. In about November, Scott was in remission and my parents took him to Florida, or tried to. Something happened with Scott and they came back. I remember being at Nanny and Papa's house, upstairs in one of the bedrooms with Scott's new dog, a black Scottish terrier named McDuff.

In early December, the doctors at Emory told Daddy they had done all they could for Scott. Daddy read in *Time* magazine about L-Asparaginase, a then-new drug used in treating certain kinds of leukemia at Sloan-Kettering Hospital in New York. Scott was accepted for treatment and off they went to New York, where they stayed until he died April 13, 1968. I remember going up to New York over the Christmas holidays. Daddy had given me a hundred dollars. The morning I was to leave, I'd carefully hidden it underneath my clothes and in my dresser drawer because I didn't want to take a purse to breakfast. While I was at breakfast, someone stole the money! I was so upset and had to call Daddy and tell him. I hated that because I knew money was really tight.

We were all in New York for the Christmas holidays in the small apartment where Mother and Daddy stayed. I remember going back and forth to the hospital every day by the subway. We had to walk quite a distance to the subway. I remember walking it with Mother and her saying: "Stay up close to the buildings and walk fast," as if someone was going to get us. I thought were many very unusual looking people on the streets of New York then—it was in the 1960s—at least very different from the people in Anniston, Alabama, and Decatur, Georgia. What do I remember about that visit to New York? I remember sitting in the waiting room and meeting a couple, the Sergeants, whose son Kenny was also at the clinic (the couple shortly thereafter had a baby boy and named it after Scott). Imagine sitting in a hospital for months watching your child die, surrounded by other parents doing the same thing. As far as I remember, there were no social workers, counselors, or support for the families.

One image from my visit to New York that Christmas is of Scott bravely going down for a bone marrow transplant, and Daddy talking about how extremely, extremely painful it was. I remember helping Scott get in a tub to take a bath and thinking how very, very thin his legs were.

We had some kind of Christmas there I guess but I don't remember anything about it. After Christmas, I went back to school. I don't remember much about those days. At spring break we went back to New York.

Scott had gotten a lot worse and I knew this would be the last time I would see him alive. I don't know if Daddy told me or if I just knew. I don't know if this is how it happened or if this is how I remembered it but I have vivid memories of the last time I saw Scott alive. I remember standing out in the hall outside Scott's room. Mother, Daddy, and Phillip and I were in the hall, and Phillip and I went in one at a time alone to see Scott. I don't remember any specifics about the conversation Scott and I had. I guess I probably blocked it from my memory. What I do remember is toward the end of the time I was with him something humorous was said (Scott had an incredible sense of humor). As I was leaving after I hugged and kissed him, which I have no memory of but I'm sure occurred, I said "Bye-bye, Sweetkins" (one of my nicknames for Scott). And he said "Bye-bye, B.B." (which is one of his nicknames for me; as a child, I was called "Bet-Bet," and it got shortened to "B.B.").

I remember closing the door and walking down the hall knowing that those final words and that final good-bye would be emblazoned in my memory forever. Daddy's poem, "They Took it with Christian Toughness," describes that last good-bye. Daddy says it well. There was no understanding this—all that was left was trust in the family verse: "Trust in the Lord with all thine heart and lean not to thine own understanding. In all thy ways, acknowledge Him and He will direct thy paths" (Proverbs 3:5-6).

I don't know how long it was between spring break and Easter when Scott died. I do remember talking with Daddy on the phone about what Phillip and I were going to do over Easter. I was planning to go stay with Nan Woodruff, my best friend from high school days, at her house in the country in Alexandria, Alabama. I remember Daddy saying: "I think we'll all be home for Easter." I knew what that meant. I remember a day or two later asking him would he please call me himself and tell me. I think that conversation happened Friday night (Good Friday) of Easter weekend when I was at Nan's house. Early Saturday morning before Easter, Black Saturday, as it is called, John Hall, the assistant minister in Anniston (where Phillip was staying) and Phillip came out to Nan's house. I don't think they called first. I just have this memory of seeing a car driving up in the long driveway to the Woodruffs' house and someone saying: "Phillip and John Hall are coming." I knew then that it was over. I don't remember much after that, other than hugging Phillip and talking with him and then talking with John Hall. There must have been some talk about going into Anniston to our house. The house where we'd all lived together so happily for all those years when Scott was alive and we didn't know what was ahead of us. Black Saturday would now have a new meaning, as would Easter. How appropriate that it happened then.

I remember going into the house and it was swarming with women from the church—cleaning up, bringing food, etc. The house hadn't been lived in since early December and it was now mid-April. I remember being in the breakfast room and hearing on the radio that Scott had died. I just remember thinking how weird it was to hear on the radio about your brother dying. I also remember that I wanted to be alone in the house and wished all those well-meaning women would just leave! Shortly thereafter, Robert, the boy I was dating at the end of high school, came by. He was in the service and was stationed somewhere away from Anniston. I think he told me his father called him and told him and he came home. I don't even know where he was stationed at the time. Anyway, he appeared and took me off in his car. I remember riding all over Golden Springs and Choccolocco (in the country outside of Anniston). Much of the time I was sitting, with the window down on the door with my upper body outside, feeling the wind blowing and the sun shining on my face. Somehow that was a soothing, calming experience. Robert had lost his mother that fall before. I remember he had written me about it, and I'd tried to be supportive of him. I guess he understood. I don't even remember what we said, if anything. I remember him taking me back home and Mrs. White, Daddy's secretary, being there. As I was walking up the stairs to my room, she said, "You and Phillip are their blessings now."

Mother and Daddy came home Saturday late-afternoon or night. I remember people coming over to the house. I remember some of my friends who came: Rodney Owens, Doyle Hyatt, and Johnny, Woody, and Nan Woodruff, as well as Jack Hollingsworth. I think Candy and Lynda Flynt, and Carolyn Medders (my first friend I had when we moved to Anniston when I was seven years old) came, too, as well as Mrs. Talley, Jane and Aunt Mick, good friends from the Church. I remember the next day was Easter. Seems like I remember we did go to church and sat in the back of the balcony and left early. I'm not even sure of that. I remember going to the funeral home that night and going in and seeing Scott. I remember something about I wanted to go in by myself and Daddy not wanting me to, or asking was I sure I wanted to go by myself. I don't remember specifically. I don't know if I went in by myself or if Daddy went with me. But I remember seeing Scott with his face so swollen from the medicine and his head so bald. I remember he had a gray-ashen color. It's a clear memory. Seems like Robert was at the funeral home too. I don't know.

The funeral was on the Monday after Easter. I remember it being a beautiful day and the church being filled. I remember seeing my friends there. I don't even know who did the funeral. I guess John Hall. I'm sure we have a bulletin from the service. I'll ask Mother and Daddy because I want to keep it. I remember going to the cemetery. There was a big tree with pink blooms, maybe a dogwood, in full bloom very close to the grave. I don't even remember the specifics of the burial. I remember more the countless times I went to the cemetery and sat at the gravestone, saying the family verse, the first part of which is on the tombstone: "Trust in the Lord with all thine heart and lean not to thine own understanding." As I read that, I'd see the initials M. S. N. (Milton Scott Noble) on the tombstone. And I'd remember my dear, smart, sweet, very alive brother with his bright face and big brown eyes always with a twinkle in them . . . as he was "before" . . . as we all were "before." A part of me is buried there too, as is the case with all of us, I'm sure. His grave is a sacred place to me.

Since then, my life has been different. After your first major loss—especially of someone so close to you—life is never the same. It's been said that one's first major loss becomes the template for how other losses are experienced. However, as painful as it was, we all experience losses, as trite as that sounds. There is a book called *Necessary Losses*. The title itself implies the universality of loss; the fact that loss is universal in no way diminishes the pain or impact of such a significant experience.

After Scott's death, I finished college as a psychology major and completed a certification program to teach elementary school. I had always been interested in children and psychology, as evidenced by the paper in my AP classes I was writing before I knew Scott was sick.

The five years in Anniston following graduation was a difficult period. Mother and Daddy and Phillip went to Cambridge, England, for that first year I was out of college. I got married in August 1971 so I didn't go with them. That was my first year of teaching, at Cooper Elementary School, with 99 percent African American enrollment. Because of Daddy's role in the civil rights movement (which you can read more about in his book, *Beyond the Burning Bus*), I had a somewhat special place at the school. I was always introduced as "Rebent Noble's daughter."

That first year I taught the second grade, with thirty-five children in the class. We had no books to speak of. I think that was about the second year that the schools had been integrated. I almost killed myself trying to teach thirty-five kids from a different culture, with no resources, while adjusting to marriage and missing my family.

I felt so alone. I often visited the cemetery which was very near my house. In addition to grieving for Scott, it was a way I could connect with my faraway family. Although I had many friends, I missed my family. It was as if someone hadn't shared that experience of loss with me, they didn't know a big part of me, and therefore I didn't really connect with them.

Scott's death gave me an extra sense of connection with those who experience loss. I remember a student named Felix in my second-grade class, who stood up during sharing time and said: "My daddy shot my mama last night." As strange as that may sound, the reality is that he did, and he shot her dead. And the child, bless his heart, was sharing it during "sharing time!" I don't know what I or the other children said or did.

The children I taught, for the most part, had so little of even the basic necessities of life. Many did not have running water or electricity.

I knew how fortunate I was in spite of the pain I was experiencing (our family has always kept me mindful of those less fortunate than we are).

After five years of teaching in Anniston, I became more interested in the school/family/community, the way it does or doesn't work together. I really wanted to go into elementary school counseling but there was no such program then. So I stumbled onto school psychology.

After completing master's and educational specialist's degrees in school psychology, I worked for three years as a school psychologist in Charleston, South Carolina. Several of the schools where I worked were on the sea islands south of Charleston: Younge's Island, John's Island, etc. Many of the children were the descendants of the original slaves who settled the islands and later became sharecroppers. On one of my first days at one of the schools the school counselor came to me and said something I initially didn't understand: "I'm coming to tell you something that's going to make your work here a lot easier. Education is not a value on this island." The impact of her words didn't hit me at first, but I soon understood what she meant, by the way the parents' responded or didn't respond to requests for school meetings about their child . . . etc. If they showed up at all for the meetings, they might arrive any time on the day of the meeting. Coming to the school meeting at all was progress. I remember offering one mother a canned drink and watching in amazement as she did not know how to open it or drink out of it. I'm not sure she'd ever had a canned drink before!

However, what this school counselor said wasn't true of everyone on the island. There was a little boy about eight or nine years old whose parents had left him (I have no idea why or where they were, nor did anyone else). The little boy lived under a car and got himself to school everyday. Can you imagine? I have a drawing he did of himself that's about an inch in size in the middle of a big sheet of paper. Does that tell you how he felt about himself? Or how significant he felt in the lives of his family? Then there was the boy who was left for dead by his father in the fields after an accident. The word was that he got axed in the head and was found by his sister who took him in for treatment. He came to school with a big bandage on his head and said to me as I was testing him: "Miz Noble, if you can just teach me how to read, I know I can get off of this island!" Education may not have been a value to many on that island but I think it was to those two boys whose stories and faces are seared into my memory. Then there was the African American principal who thanked me for all the energy I put into my work at his school. He said words I'll never forget about other people in Charleston who thought the children at the island schools were "behind the back of God"—in other words, not even God values them. Imagine feeling like that! I spent several years working in the island schools with a population that was one or two steps from the situations described so beautifully in Pat Conroy's book, *The Water Is Wide*, about Daufuskie Island, South Carolina. Later a movie, *Conrack* (the children couldn't say "Conroy"), was made of this book. Those were years spent working with what would have been described in earlier days as "those less fortunate . . ." Now students receive free college loans, etc., as incentives to work in such situations.

While in Charleston, about 1978 or 1979, I attended a conference on children and divorce. The conference was not a scientific research-based presentation but featured a clinician talking about his experiences. I remember someone in the audience asked the question: "Is divorce necessarily bad (devastating) for all children?" or something to that effect. I am not being dramatic when I say that bells went off in my head. My initial internal response was: "Well of course!" followed by "Maybe . . ." and then a very thoughtful "I don't know . . ." (that experience was extremely significant for me, and I knew then that when I went back to get my Ph.D., my dissertation would be on children and divorce). I experienced almost like a calling to help children of divorce and their families. I'm sure my own divorce in 1976 had something to do with my decision to research children of divorce. I'd often thought if this divorce was as hard as it was for me, even though I was the one who wanted it and I was a twenty-six-year-old adult, how much more devastating it must be for children.

I went on to graduate school and did five years of research and writing my dissertation on children and divorce. My research investigated the relation between children's understanding of divorce, their individual attribution styles, and their adjustment at school. The research question grew out of my interest in the concept of resilience, hardiness, locus of control—in short, personality variables that mediate adjustment, the very topic I was researching in my high school AP class when Daddy told me about Scott's illness. This research question is just another way to ask or investigate how one copes with tragedy. The whole notion/concept of loss includes both death and divorce as well as numerous other forms of loss that individuals experience. My dissertation is dedicated to Scott, as well as to my parents and my grandfather who at that time was almost one hundred (he lived to be one hundred and six). The dedication reads:

> This dissertation is dedicated to my parents, Betty and Phil Noble, who have served as a constant source of support, strength, wisdom and guidance over the years. The ever-present, undying support, pride, humor, love, and encouragement has sustained me through my daily life. I cherish them both

for who they are, for the numerous sacrifices they have made, and for the countless opportunities they have provided for me throughout my life.

I also want to acknowledge my grandfather, Mr. Milton C. Scott, and "almost centenarian" who has provided a very positive role model of health, faith, humor, and persistence and to thank him for his generosity over the years.

Finally, I want to acknowledge my brother, Scott Noble, whose brave struggle with leukemia taught me much about living.

After graduate school, I came to Atlanta to start a private practice and shortly thereafter began teaching part-time at two liberal arts colleges, Oglethorpe University and Agnes Scott College. I'd had a difficult time deciding what I wanted to do after graduate school because I wanted to do it all: research, teaching, private practice. When I was deciding about a couple of academic jobs, which I later turned down much to the dismay of some of my professors, the deciding factor was that I wanted to work with children. If I went the academic route, I'd have much less opportunity to do that, at least for a number of years until I had survived the tenure system. Initially, I began teaching at Oglethorpe University in the education and psychology departments and after about a year or two, the head of the psychology department came to me and asked me to develop a seminar on any topic of particular interest to me. This was within a few years shortly after I had finished my dissertation, and of course I wanted to do the seminar on children and divorce; however, I realized that the topic was too narrow, and I was probably the only one that would have enough interest in children and divorce to be willing to devote a whole semester to its study. So I broadened the topic to children and stress. My dissertation had investigated children of divorce under the rubric of divorce as a stressful life event and I'd done much research in the area of children and stress for my dissertation. The course investigated numerous stressors that children might experience in their lives, such as death, divorce, adoption, child abuse, alcoholism of the parents, natural disasters, hospitalization/chronic illness, and violence/war and how adults in the children's environment, both professionals, counselors, teachers, school psychologists, as well as parents, might intervene to help minimize the effects of the stressors. The essence of the course is helping children deal with those very stressful, often unexpected events, which may be just another way to say helping children cope with tragedy in their lives. One student, in evaluating the course, wrote words that were gratefully appreciated: "The net result of teaching a course like this one is that you release a crack team of child advocates upon the world. There are much worse things."

I've also taught since 1990 at my alma mater Agnes Scott College. The course I've taught the most is on working with special needs children. As a part of the class, I have speakers come and share their experience with the future teachers. The speakers are either teachers who teach children with that disability or students themselves who have lived the disability. I've had speakers on topics such as learning disability, visually impaired, hearing impaired, mentally retarded, etc. One student with Down's syndrome, Katie, who began talking in my class when she was twelve years old and is now twenty-two, has spoken to the class on numerous occasions. I'll never forget Katie and the impact she's had on my life as well as many of the other students. A student who heard her speak wrote this as a reflection on the experience:

"There's no doubt in my soul that Katie Wilson has sealed

my fate to attempt to change the world. As a young woman with Down's syndrome, she possesses more strength than many of us will ever have. Her perspective on the world is refreshing and yet heavy. She's a person with feelings and heartaches, a person who truly understands what love is and what love is not. And yet, Katie still manages to embrace the world lovingly with open arms. When she spoke in our class, she made me sob uncontrollably. My tears were not of pity but of pure inspiration. She is the model student, a student who wants to learn and appreciates those who teach her. It would be unfair for me to try to verbally (or in the written word) articulate how she changed my life. Words just cannot describe how Katie helped me to put my life as a person and as a future educator into perspective. We truly should embrace each day and live it to the fullest."

Katie continues to be an inspiration in my life as well, especially on the hard days.

In my private practice, in addition to focusing on learning disabilities and attention deficit hyperactivity disorder, I have also specialized in children of divorce. I prefer to work with couples in the beginning stages of the separation/divorce in order that I might guide them through the process in ways that will minimize the potential negative effects for their children. I also work with the children using play therapy or other therapeutic approaches. I remember I was very excited when I managed to scrape together fifty dollars the first Christmas after getting my Ph.D. to buy myself my first children of divorce game. I had an image of me sitting on the floor of an office playing that game with children of divorce, an image which was probably a strong contributing factor to my decision to go into private practice, as opposed to full-time academics. Through the years I've worked with numerous families that are divorcing. What a challenge it has been to stay focused on ways to help the child and "stay the course" amidst all "the stuff" that is there with angry, hurt, revenge-seeking parents who are, despite the conflict between ex-spouses, trying to help their child.

In private practice I've also ended up working to some extent with loss in general. Several families come to mind that have lost children either through miscarriages, birth problems, or by tragic accidents. I'll never forget working with the family whose son was killed tragically when he was in college. I'd tested their son two times over the years initially in about fourth grade and later in high school. He was an amazing young man, with attention deficit and hyperactivity disorder (ADHD), who'd even helped me make a presentation to teachers in a workshop about working with ADHD in the classroom. In working with his parents I saw and experienced firsthand the depths of despair and the emotional trauma parents go through in the loss of a child. My past experience with my family during Scott's illness and death certainly helped me as I tried to be with this couple in the midst of their pain and seeking for answers.

You the reader may wonder why I am telling you all of this. At the end of Daddy's introduction to the poem "Carvings" and in the sermon "Tragedy and the Will of God," he says that "perhaps God can use [his sharing of his experience in this book] to help some others in their deep hurt." Although I already knew it on some levels, in writing this reflection, I am struck by how the themes of resilience, hardiness, coping, loss, run through all of my work. My loss of Scott may have been used to help others as they struggled with unexpected events, whether loss in the form of divorce or death, the routine stressors of life, or the unexpected, catastrophic events that happen, or the loss of the dream of having a perfect child to the reality of having a special-needs child.

Perhaps all of these professional experiences have been a way I have worked through my own personal experience of the painful loss of Scott at such an early age. Maybe in some way my work has been a tribute to him and all that he meant to me.

As I draw this reflection to a close, I am again at a loss for what to say. Once again, I'm sitting here with a wet paper, weeping softly, as I struggle to try and sum up in words what this experience has meant for my life. It is so deep and central to who I am. My life has been shaped so much by Scott's death that I indeed am a very different person than I would have been without that experience. His loss has affected me deeply in so many ways, both personally and professionally. I can't imagine that my life would be my life without this experience. It has probably been the experience that has shaped my life more than any other, that loss and growing up in the wonderful family that I did. Perhaps reading Daddy's poems and sermons in this book will give you a sense of our wonderful family. How much I wish that we could have and would share more of our memories of Scott. Not that we don't talk about him—we do. But somehow we know, and it especially hit me as I read Daddy's poems, the pain is so deep that in Daddy's words, "some depths can never be shared" [Introduction].

Throughout difficult times in my own life—my own ovarian cancer, the loss of a very significant relationship, my mother's recent and ongoing debilitating illness—two verses have been very significant and have sustained me. Agnes Irvine Scott, my great-great-great grandmother on my mother's side, for whom Agnes Scott College is named, passed on what through the generations became the family verse, Proverbs 3:5-6, which says: "Trust in the Lord with all thine heart and lean not to thine own understanding. In all thy ways, acknowledge Him and He will direct thy paths." I sewed these verses in needlepoint for my family several years ago. From Daddy, I've come to treasure the verse he mentions in the sermon and in this book: "We know that in everything God works together for good for those who love him and who are called according to his purpose" (Romans 8:28 RSV). Both of these verses have supported me through difficult times in my life. I say them every morning as a part of my early morning devotional/meditation.

I wear two rings: my Agnes Scott College ring, and a ring from my father's mother who died when my father was two years old, probably of ovarian cancer. The rings are daily reminders of the two verses, one from my mother's family and one from my father's family. The verses give me strength as I live my daily life and remind me of the heritage of faith for generations that I have, as Daddy would say, "coursing through my veins." To those two heritages, I add another: the heritage of Scott, the heritage of his spirit that has enriched and shaped my life in so many ways (See poem, "We Have this Heritage"). But even as I've written all of this, I know that to some extent the impact of Scott's death and its meaning for my life is incapable of being described. I just feel it, and I know it's with me everyday. His spirit is also there with those who knew him. I always feel there's a special connection when I see his friends and/or those who knew him, especially Terry Braxton. And I know they feel it, too. It's almost like a very special presence we share and remember as we hug each other in greeting.

I am fortunate to have my heritage from both sides of my family, the Scotts and the Nobles, as represented by the two verses. Those two very significant heritages are bridged together by the heritage of Scott and his remarkably courageous spirit. His spirit will be with me always and will continue to be a source of strength as I live the rest of my life, through whatever else comes . . . until I see him again one day and look at that bright face with that tousled brown hair and those big, brown eyes filled with gentle love and humor, feel his arms around me and hear Scott say, in only the way he can: "What took you so long, B.B.!" Until then, I have this heritage . . . and what a heritage it is!

# FROM SCOTT'S BROTHER

The whole idea of this book is unorthodox—a family writing about something intensely personal with the perspective of thirty-five plus years in the hope that they may have something of value or meaningful to say for others.

When my father first raised the idea of my sister and me writing pieces for this book, I immediately said yes without thinking, without any idea as to what I would write. After many weeks of wrestling with this and trying to express something of real value, in one sense, I have given up. What was emerging seemed too much like trite platitudes and empty sentiment.

Instead, I have simply recounted some ideas and insights that have developed meaning for me in the hope that they will have meaning to others. I know that I speak for the rest of my family in saying that we offer these thoughts and words—with all their flaws and perhaps their vain emptiness—in the simple sincere hope that in some small way they will ease others' struggles and pain.

We humbly ask you to accept these words in this spirit.

## Tragedy Plus Thirty-Five Years

Tragedy is a jumble. It is not just one thing but a jumble of many different things, most of which we have never experienced before, or at least not in such intensity. We simply don't know how to deal with it all. It is obviously intense personal pain, but it often includes joyful memories, massive confusion, blind rage, fear of the unknown, sympathy for others, feelings of guilt and regret, age-old issues of God and mortality, and on and on it goes. The sheer complexity and enormity overwhelms us.

How do we react? What do we do? How *do* we *get beyond* tragedy?

In the short term—whatever works.

Each person's tragedy is intensely personal—indeed each tragedy is unique. No one else has the same relationship or experiences with tragedy, and each person's psyche is different; indeed their emotions and family circumstances, their very beings, are all unique.

We all get past tragedies in our own ways. Each day, whether they are days of tragedy or just our everyday lives, sometimes good, sometimes bad—we all as individuals have developed psychic and social mechanisms that enable us to get by.

Sometimes life is easy and we have a great sense of its daily joy; sometimes it seems that it is all an overwhelming, crushing burden and it's more than we can bear.

But no matter how bad things get, somehow we get through to the end of the day without jumping off a bridge or just going mad.

Many years ago I read an interview with Jackie Gleason that has stuck with me. To the world Gleason was a happy and successful man who brought great joy and laugher to many. Privately, he was a tortured soul who fought his private demons every day.

Gleason's childhood was a catalogue of poverty, pain, rejection, and loss. As an adult, in his personal life tragedy and pain were never far away. Professionally, he had been largely a failure at night clubs, radio, movies, and earlier attempts at television. But he persisted and took enormous risks. In reality, each of Gleason's brilliantly funny television performances was a personal psychic triumph over tragedy and insecurity.

From surface appearances, one could dismiss Gleason as just a good entertainer, a funny man. But, he was much more than just a great comedian; he was a bold innovator and pioneer in the early days of television. In the 1950s, no one really knew how to use this radical new box of cold electrons and lifeless vacuum tubes to communicate ideas and complex human emotions to millions of people all at the same time.

For Gleason, every television episode was in essence a trauma— a public experiment risking personal failure, rejection—"Am I funny; will they laugh at this joke; will this work on TV?" Doubt and insecurity were constant.

And it wasn't just the performing; he did it all—scripts, music, producing, directing—he invented TV comedy. He took huge risks and he did it every Saturday night at 7 pm—live, no edits, no retakes, no focus groups or phony laugh tracks.

He prevailed over his own personal tragedies and produced triumphs. And just how good was he? His nicknames were "The Great One" and "King of Television."

How he did it: "Booze, a broad or a prayer—whatever gets me through the night." That was his formula for survival.

Something within makes us want to reject the seemingly weak indulgences of "booze" or "a broad" and say it should be a prayer. This sounds good and appeals to our sense of propriety. But I think Gleason was right on a fundamental level. To Gleason, "booze" or "a broad" were shorthand for something more basic—diversions and companionship.

We have all seen those who seek diversion immediately after tragedy. They throw themselves into their work; they begin to drink heavily or do drugs to dull their pain, their senses, and their memories. Clearly, most of us would say that excessive work is better than excessive booze or other destructive diversion.

And Gleason's "a broad"—I think that's really about people and not sex—it's about leaning on others to get through it. Be it talking, sharing, listening or whatever—people can help in the process of dealing with tragedy but eventually they leave, too. Such is the nature of things.

Regardless of the diversions, the pains and questions will remain, though perhaps diminished a bit, after the diversion is over. Ultimately, we must face things. After it all, we are left on our own to deal with tragedy and sort through what it means in our own lives.

I use Gleason's story as an extreme example of the fundamental truth that we all do what we have to do to survive and then, if possible, we minimize the damage that we do to ourselves in surviving. Gleason's method was self-destructive and may well have shortened his life with what folks call bad living, but it worked for him in the sense that it got him through his nights. It enabled him to survive. Some of us are able to turn tragedy into triumph by using pain as a catalyst to do something positive. Gleason brought laughter and great comedic insight to many and personally he was known as a compassionate and generous person—but his public triumphs came at a great private price.

In the end, it comes down to us as individuals. Do we, as

William Faulkner said in another context, "not simply endure but prevail"?

## Tragedy has a Price

Over the years I have developed my own "toothpaste tube" theory of human personality and response. In most ways we are generally similar in our life experiences—home and family, school and growing up, developing to maturity. In different cultures and at different levels of economic wealth the details of our experiences are different but the rough patterns are the same. We may be Crest or Colgate but it's all a tube of toothpaste.

But for some of us, extraordinary events or circumstances have a big and unusual impact—we are born wealthy, are sexually molested as children, have great musical or intellectual gifts, suffer massive losses or tragedies, or have fabulous opportunities. Whatever the extraordinary stimulus, we seem to react in some equally extraordinary way. As with pushing on a tube of toothpaste—there is an impact or effect in some way—the extraordinary response or consequence may be for good or for ill, but it will show itself one way or the other, somewhere, somehow.

Beyond my simple pop-psychology theories, I don't know what are the determining factors between tragedy spurring us to triumphs or on to further despair. There seem to be many cases of things going both ways. I am sure some have spent many years trying to understand why. I simply accept that we do react differently.

For many of us, simple survival is about all that we can achieve, and getting beyond the tragedy to a triumph just does not happen very often—so be it. But perhaps it should happen more often and I do believe that most of us can achieve some type of our own personal triumph. Some have suggested that the way to get past the tragedy to the triumph is by focusing on others and trying to do something good in the lives of others. But I only know what worked for me.

## What Worked for Me

On one level what I did, how I got by it is unimportant—it's simply what worked for me in my life and my circumstances. I responded uniquely to my own history, life, and circumstances. Another trite platitude: each of us is unique and the way we respond is unique. The way I "handled it" had many implications for my future life, some good and bad.

I am a Scots-Irish Calvinist, full-blooded on both my mother's and father's side. We are solitary, stubborn stoics—perhaps genetically comfortable in the desolate emptiness of the Scotland. We are the penultimate expression on this planet of a race of tight-assed white people.

When Scott died I was seventeen years old and I was alone at a military school. Scott had been my best friend, in a real sense my only really good friend, and I've never had another since.

I went through it essentially alone. Doing it alone was the catalyst and the molder of my solitary character. I came to terms with myself and I am comfortable being alone.

The times were the late 1960s, the times of rebellion, rock 'n' roll and doing your own thing. I did mine; I still do. Simon and Garfunkel were a great comfort. Creative brooding felt good. Perhaps to others I am selfish; maybe I am. But I have survived.

But most of all, I thought. I spent endless hours looking out the windows, gazing into space and quietly exploring the deep and dark recesses of my mind. I thought about everything that a seventeen-year-old could think about. With the pseudo-profundity of late adolescence, I thought about the grand immortal questions of the infinite universe to the intimate personal and private pains that have never crossed my lips.

I have tried to continue and think broadly and deeply about some things—in reality just a few things of my daily work. I am keenly aware of my limitations. I know that in terms of raw brain power I don't have much to offer. But I do know how to think aggressively, be persistent, to take risks, to push the bounds of the ordinary into the creative and imaginative—though I don't have the intellectual power to push it to the realm of the truly original.

What limited success I have had in my professional life has come from my understanding of these insights that I gained.

My solitary nature is not all good or bad but just what is. I am sure that my solitary ways have had ill effects for my wife, my marriage, and my own family life with children.

And, what has come of all my solitary ways and thinking on the subject of tragedy?

I have found a few simple truths—at least they are true to me. To those that are still suffering from raw wounds, these so-called truths will no doubt sound simplistic. I am sure if they had been offered to me when I was in the raw and suffering state, I too would have rejected them out of hand with suitable indignation and rage.

But yet, here they are. Offered as simple "truths" that I believe only because they have meaning for me.

**The pain is not permanent.** The simple but profound reality is that we do get beyond it in time—some way, somehow, each of us does get beyond at least the immediate pain.

People around us seem too quick with what seem like trite phrases of sympathy. "I'm so sorry. I know how you feel." "You will get over it in time." "This too shall pass." "Time heals all things." "What doesn't kill you makes you stronger."

We resist when we first hear these words. They seem like phony sentimentality. At the initial time of pain they seem to hurt more than help, but it is just people trying to reach out and help. In their own inadequate and human way, they don't know what else to do.

And, they are right, we will get past it. We do not die.

But we don't want to hear any of this at the time.

Once it happens, the tragedy itself is never gone; it becomes a part of us. But we do get beyond the immediate pain of the event. Somehow our soul and psyche do allow the pain to diminish, perhaps simply because we could not live for long with such an intense level of hurt. Just as a flesh wound eventually heals and the pain goes away, the scars are always there.

We get beyond it only in the sense that we move on, our life continues and we do survive.

**Tragedy warps our perspective and often debilitates us, but the world goes on and in time we will rejoin the world.** Because tragedy is by definition an extraordinary event—it does not happen to us every day—our perspective is warped. It overwhelms us; our tragedy is huge.

Others seem unaffected. How can this be? How can others be so unaffected?

As I write this the news reports are coming in of the Asian tsunami disaster. Over 150,000 dead. Some estimates are that perhaps over five million people will in some way suffer from the immediate and long term impact. Five million people—but yet I sit here simply tapping selfish thoughts on my laptop. How could that be? How could I be so callous?

Over a million died in Rwanda a few years ago. I did nothing. In our living memory of the last hundred years, tens of millions have died in useless human carnage in Germany, China, Russia—pick a place, any place—and there were countless dead and senseless suffering.

Tell me again, what was your tragedy?

If you are freshly wounded this sounds cold and crass; it is not intended to hurt you. But for me, it was actually a comfort in that it made my pain seem to fade the more I pondered past tragedies of such historic proportions.

## My Well

For me the most enduring metaphor is that of an ancient well in a parched desert. Eight years after Scott died, I spent about a year wandering the world alone, mostly in the deserts of the Middle East. Once, I came across an old and ancient well, its age probably measured in thousand-year spans. The well was deep and looking in you could not see water, simply a deep, black hole.

Above ground the well had a circular stone wall base about four feet high and along the wall were deep cuts twelve to eighteen inches deep—gashes in solid rock worn by hundreds of years of ropes pulling heavy skins or buckets of water from deep within the earth.

For countess years, countless people have thrown their skins, jugs and buckets over the stone wall and into the deep, black hole. And then, they pulled their ropes across the wall, drawing up the water to sustain their life and purpose—and wearing away an imperceptible bit of the stone wall that contained the well.

There was no name on the well. Best I could tell, no one owned it and no one seemed to control it. It was simply there. People came to it and took water for drinking, watering crops, cooking, cleaning—all the things required to simply sustain their lives. For people, for animals, for all tribes and ages and races—it was simply there.

Some might see the well essentially as a *good thing* that nourished and sustained life, and indeed it does. But, I saw it differently. I saw the well, like human tragedy, as an essential part of life. It is a given—there is no life without tragedy. There is no life without water.

The question for us is what we do with what we get from the well?

What do we do? How do we react? What happens next?

To me, my tragedy, my simple little tragedy of one person at one time—has become like that well—something common shared with countless generations since time immemorial. It is a shared experience with the faceless humanity of the ages. I have gone back to the well countless times. Again and again I have dropped my bucket over the wall into the deep, dark hole.

The water has served many purposes for me; I have received many things from the well. It has given me strength. It has given me perspective. It has given me hope. It has reminded me that countless others have been there before and shared the waters of the well.

It has taught me that nothing I have pulled up from the depths of the darkness is special or unique. The same water has been pulled up by others for untold years in the past and others will do the same for untold years to come.

I am not special or unique—I'm only unique in what I choose to do with my water from the well, what I make of my life.

My well of tragedy is where I go to touch my core, the place where I find my basics. Sometimes I even go back to the well for what is not there. Looking into the empty darken reflection of the well, I see what never was.

They say that soldiers and others who lose a limb have sensations that their hand or foot is still there though they know it isn't. I sometimes go to the well to get that sensation, that sense of what was lost. I think of Scott as my missing limb—the lifelong best friend that I didn't get to have for all of life.

I occasionally think what I would say to him. Beginning many years ago when I first began wandering those deserts alone, I have often thought of sharing the experiences with him—but he wasn't there. To this day I remember sitting on a dry rocky hill looking over the edge into the vast empty desert—not knowing what would come as I thought about venturing forth. I thought of how in our young days together we often said "my hard fist and his good brain could get us out of most anything." He wasn't there. I sat and cried. And then, off I went alone.

The well of Scott's tragedy has given me a jumble of insights and ideas, pains and problems, inspirations and hopes, character formers and traits. It has become a familiar place I return to over and over—often not with a specific need but simply the need to tread the comfortable path back to the well. Each time I put my bucket down . . .

In reading this you may feel that there is a lack of passion or emotion here. You are probably right. Over the years I have channeled my passion into thought—the pain has become reflection and the longings have become lessons. This is written without the power that I am sure is in my father's words or the pain that I am sure is felt by my sister and mother.

I don't suggest my seeming lack of passion is either good or bad, but simply it reflects what I have learned and how I have gotten beyond the tragedy.

## Alone

With me, the one lasting sensation has been a profound sense of being alone—an acceptance of aloneness forever. Nothing has ever filled the void.

As time passed, the fact that I did get through it—alone—became a great source of strength to me. I love people and I relish the interaction and truly hunger for more. But ultimately I am content alone. I got through death alone. I can get through life alone.

And what of God, of faith, of strength and refuge and all those things that sound so good and one would expect to hear from the son of a preacherman thinking about such things?

It's all there, in different words and different ideas and seen in different ways. But it is all there.

I did believe then that I was not alone—that there was Another (though in the Arabian desert they called Another by a different name). I do not feel alone now; I talk with Another every day.

There were things that came from Scott's death that had meaning and power and insight in my life. Those things have given me strength and drive and a purpose that is real to me.

Through it all the quiet optimism of my parents and sister and the sincere resolute spirit that "We have been so blessed" is still a marvel to me. It has pushed me to think and act more broadly, more deeply, and with more reverence and focus.

Have I used these gifts well, have I done justice to what I have been given, and all those other questions that we as Christians are compelled to ask ourselves about such things? I really do not know. I will leave it to others to judge.

I know that it has given me the hope to try to achieve, to do something bigger and beyond my self, to not give up when things are hard.

Those are the simple—and perhaps trite—truths that have come to me, that have given my life more vitality and hope. These have been my own small triumphs out of tragedy.

For me, it is enough . . . and I thank God for it everyday.

*Appendix*

# Memorials to Scott

Scott's untimely death and the way he handled his sickness and suffering made a marked and deep impression on his peers. There were four significant expressions of the impact he made.

## The Troop

Scott died on April 13, 1968, and the following tribute was written by the members of his Scout Troop five days later:

> A Tribute to Star Scout Scott Noble
>
> When we try to write a tribute to Scott Noble we realize, more than ever before, his short life meant so much to us.
>
> Star Scout Scott Noble left us an everlasting image of good leadership. His desire to go camping and his camping skills were far above the average.
>
> Scott had received the God and Country Award and displayed the qualities of Christian character and good citizenship in all of our associations with him.
>
> God in his infinite wisdom called Scott away, but his memory and example will live forever with the boys and leaders of Troop 7.

## The Sunday School Class

Scott was a member of the Sunday School class for those in the seventh and eighth grades of the First Presbyterian Church, Anniston, Alabama. On the first anniversary of his death, April 13, 1969 the class was named the "Scott Noble Class." This resolution was written by the members of the class. On the wall in the class room there hangs a picture of Scott and the resolution hangs underneath it.

### SCOTT NOBLE RESOLUTION

We the members of the 7th and 8th grade Sunday School Class of the First Presbyterian Church of Anniston, Alabama, resolve this day, April 13, 1969, to name our class the "Scott Noble Class."

We remember Scott as a member of our group, who studied and played and lived with us. We remember him in many ways—as the left-handed first baseman on his Little League baseball team, the quarterback of his football team—really a natural athlete and great sports fan; we remember that he was a Star Scout in Troop 7 who earned the "God and Country" award, that he took piano lessons, built model rockets, liked to hunt, collected coins; we remember that he was a very good student who particularly enjoyed Social Studies and that he was interested in politics and helped to distribute campaign literature in one election; we remember that he was a great tease who could mimic his father and the family cook with equal skill in dialect and that he was an excellent storyteller with a keen sense of humor; remember that he was fun to be with, not perfect all the time, but very human like the rest of us; we remember that he was cheerful and courageous in suffering, and that he had committed his life to Christ.

We resolve to name this group the "Scott Noble Class" because we loved Scott as a person and he loved us in return, because we wish to honor his memory, and because we hope it will remind us and this congregation of the tremendous gift of eternal life in Jesus Christ.

## The School Honor Award

The Scott Noble Honor Award was established in 1969 at Johnston Junior High School where Scott was a student. Each year a student is selected to receive the Award who best exemplifies the characteristics of Scott. The criteria for selecting the Award recipient is in the following profile written by members of a student committee:

> The student is Christian in belief and practice. He is friendly, loyal, and dependable. He is thoughtful and considerate, strives for excellence in his schoolwork and participates enthusiastically in sports, has a happy disposition and a respect for others, which further characterize him. His maturity of spirit is reflected in his inner discipline and in his ability to bear hardships without complaining.

The Award was continued each year until with the changes in the Anniston School system, Johnston Junior High School no longer existed.

## Scott Noble Memorial Chapel

Scott was an enthusiastic member of the Scout Troop of the First Presbyterian Church in Anniston, Alabama. For several summers he went to Scout Camp at the Comer Scout Reservation of the Choccolocco Council of the Boy Scouts of America. In the summer of 1967, when he was battling leukemia, he was an active participant at Scout Camp. He died at Easter time, April 13, 1968.

In 1971, with funds that were given as memorials to Scott and other contributions from the First Presbyterian Church and friends, the Choccolocco Council of the Boy Scouts of America, built a chapel at Camp Comer and dedicated it on June 27 as the "Scott Noble Memorial Chapel." The bronze plaque on the Chapel reads:

ERECTED IN LOVING MEMORY OF
MILTON SCOTT NOBLE
Star Scout of Troop 7, God and Country Award
Camp Comer 1966 and 1967, Christian in spirit and
Character, excellent student, all-around athlete
Died of leukemia, Easter, April 13, 1968
Son of Rev. and Mrs. J. Phillips Noble
First Presbyterian Church, Anniston, Alabama

Chapel given by Charles A. Hamilton, Arthur M. Lee, and
other friends of the family
In memory of this outstanding scout who exemplified
scouting's highest ideals

Scott's picture and the following text were printed in the
dedication program:

MILTON SCOTT NOBLE

Milton Scott Noble was born December 15, 1954, in Greenville, S.C., the son of Rev. and Mrs. J. Phillips Noble. With his
parents and sister, Betty, and brother, Phillips, Jr., he moved to
Anniston, Alabama, in 1956. With the exception of his first 20
months, he lived his entire life in Anniston.

The first six years of school were spent at Woodstock Elementary School. During this time, in addition to top grades,
he played Little League baseball, basketball and football. During
the sixth grade, he was selected as the all-star quarterback from
all the city's Little League teams.

In January of 1967, it was discovered that he had lymphosarcoma. An operation followed. Radiation removed the

cancer, but on March 30, 1967, it was discovered that he had leukemia. Treatment for this was taken in and out of hospitals until Christmas of 1967.

During the year of 1967, Scott continued most of his normal activities, even including Little League baseball in the spring, and a week of Scout camp at Comer during which time he participated in competitive athletic events. He entered Johnston Junior High in September.

At Christmas in 1967, he was taken to Memorial Hospital in New York for treatment, because of the possibility of a "break-through" with a particular new drug which had generated hope for leukemia patients. With the exception of a brief ten-day period when he was able to be out of the hospital, he remained for four months in Memorial Hospital where he died at age 13 on Black Saturday, April 13, 1968. He was buried on Easter Monday in Anniston, Alabama.

During the time of great suffering from the slow disease of leukemia and the discomforts of the treatment, Scott showed remarkably mature qualities of courage, determination and faith. He took the unavoidable suffering with this attitude, expressed in his own words: "What you can't help, you just have to take." His long confinement did not reduce him to complaints and despair, but with a steady and hopeful faith, he faced the experience with courage and determination.

The Dedication Litany was also printed in the program:

Leader: To the glory of the living God, who became flesh and dwelt among us, and we beheld his grace and truth,
People: We dedicate this Chapel, O God.
Leader: To the worship of the living God, who to this day

enters human hearts and lives, to redeem, forgive, love and inspire,

People: We dedicate this Chapel, O God.

Leader: To the end that young boys may catch the vision of the living God, and be inspired to live for Him during their days on earth,

People: We dedicate this Chapel, O God.

Leader: To the end that young boys may learn the qualities of character that make for true greatness, such as humility, faithfulness, honesty, and love for fellowman,

People: We dedicate this Chapel, O God.

Leader: To the end that young men may learn how to face difficult and painful experiences with courage and determination, strengthened by faith,

People: We dedicate this Chapel, O God.

Leader: To the end that youth and adults who worship here may catch the deep meaning of human life, and gain courage for the facing of death,

People: We dedicate this Chapel, O God.

Leader: To the praise of Almighty God,

And for the inspiration and good

Of all who shall ever come here;

And in loving memory of Milton Scott Noble,

One of God's gallant young men,

People: We dedicate this Chapel of beauty and inspiration, O God.

# ACKNOWLEDGMENTS

This book was a long time in the making. The poetry came in the days, weeks, and months when Scott was fighting leukemia and in the months that followed after his death. The essay, Tragedy and the Will of God, came much later, some thirty years later. Tragedy nearly always brings the "God question." Where is God in the tragedy? It is a huge and complicated question and quick and simple and trite answers are never satisfactory.

Through the years of being with people in tragedy and facing over and again the "God question" I gradually found some help with the question which resulted in this essay. It still does not give total answers and certainly does not show much patience with easy, glib and trite answers that are all too often given. But the thought expressed in it has helped me to deal better with the supreme tragedy of the death of a child. Others who have read or heard the essay spoken have also found some help through it.

The three pieces from Scott's Mother, Sister and Brother are the most recent ones. Once the book took shape and form, I thought it would be significant for the other three members of the family who also went through the experience of Scott's suffering and death to express their thoughts and feelings and record how the experience had affected their lives.

I am deeply grateful to all three for doing the hard task of writing their response to Scott's suffering and death. It gives the broader expression of a families handling of the event rather than just the way I handled it. The family's response will touch in a better way the lives of mothers, sisters and brothers than just the response of a father.

I owe a large debt of gratitude to numerous people who were a strong support to our whole family during this time of trial. The congregation of the First Presbyterian Church rallied around us with much expressed love and support. When we went to Sloan Kettering Hospital in New York because it appeared that a breakthrough for curing leukemia might be coming, the church accepted my being in New York for almost five months. Not only that but they were generous in seeing that funds were available to meet our expenses during that time.

I am grateful to my long time friend from Seminary days, Will Ormond, who after first reading the poems said they ought to be published. They are being published thirty seven years later, and a couple of years after Will died.

When the time came for putting the book in its final form the staff at NewSouth was a significant help. The editor Randall Williams took a very personal interest in the book and his good editing had its usual good impact on the book. Brian Seidman, the managing editor, helped in many significant ways.

Of course, no help was greater than that of my wife of sixty years, Betty Pope Scott Noble and my daughter, Betty Scott, and son, Phil Noble, Jr. Without their support and encouragement the book would never have come into being. We all offer it in the hope that others will find some inspiration and help in their lives as they face their tragedies.

—J. PHILLIPS NOBLE

THE NOBLE FAMILY, 2005
*Phil Sr., Betty Scott, Phil Jr., Betty Pope Scott*

# TABLE OF POEMS

The poetry sections:

The poems, alphabetically by title: